DATE DUE

~~OC 6 '95~~		
MR 1 '96		
~~AV 25 '96~~		
~~SE 26 '96~~		
~~AG 4 '97~~		
~~OC 27 '97~~		
AP 2 '04		
~~JY 3 06~~		

GOLF, PLAIN AND SIMPLE

GOLF, PLAIN AND SIMPLE

Let the "Swing Surgeon"
Make You a Better Golfer

by Don Trahan

with illustrations by
Ken Lewis

Technical Consultant: John Andrisani

HarperPerennial
A Division of HarperCollins*Publishers*

This book was previously published in 1986 by Quinlan Press. It is here reprinted by arrangement with the author.

HarperCollins books may be purchased for educational, business, or sales promotional use. For information, please call or write: Special Markets Department, HarperCollins Publishers, Inc., 10 East 53rd Street, New York, NY 10022. Telephone: (212) 207-7528; Fax: (212) 207-7222.

First HarperPerennial edition published 1992.

Library of Congress Cataloging-in-Publication Data

Trahan, Don
    Golf, plain and simple : let the swing surgeon make you a better
golfer / by Don Trahan. — 1st HarperPerennial ed.
        p.   cm.
    ISBN 0-06-097431-1 (alk. paper)

    1. Golf.   I. Title.
GV965.T724   1992
796.352—dc20   91-50509

92 93 94 95 96 RRD 10 9 8 7 6 5 4 3 2 1

To my mother and father for introducing me to this great game and for providing me with the opportunity to play as a junior. And to my wife Susan for her tireless support throughout my career as a PGA professional and during the writing of this book.

Don Trahan, known as ''The Swing Surgeon,'' is the Director of Instruction at Sea Pines Plantation, Harbour Town Golf Links, Hilton Head Island. A PGA pro since 1972, he was a member of Georgia's PGA Challenge Cup team for seven years. Trahan is a *GOLF Magazine* teaching editor, as well as the creator of COMPU-GOLF, one of the only computer software instruction programs for golf in the world. He has given over 30,000 individual lessons, instructing a range of players from PGA Tour members to weekend amateurs. Trahan considers himself the average golfer's best friend, shaving thousands of strokes during his career.

John Andrisani is a senior editor for *GOLF Magazine* and former assistant editor of the British-based *Golf Illustrated*, the world's oldest weekly golf publication. With 1985 British Open champion Sandy Lyle, he is author of *Learning Golf: The Lyle Way,* and he is currently working on an instructional book with golfing superstar Seve Ballesteros. He has worked with Don Trahan on several articles for *GOLF.* A recent holder of the American Golf Writers' Championship, Andrisani plays off a 5-handicap at Siwanoy Country Club in Westchester County, New York.

Ken Lewis, recognized as one of the world's leading illustrators of the golf swing, trained at Britain's Southend School of Art, and became a freelancer in 1978. His work has appeared in several major books and he is currently the chief contributing artist for *GOLF Magazine.* He is married to professional golfer Beverly Lewis.

Contents

Introduction

I am unabashedly in love with the game of golf. I have been playing for twenty-five years, since the age of eleven. I competed successfully at top amateur levels before becoming a PGA professional in 1972. Since then, in addition to continuing to compete successfully, I have earned my keep teaching the game to countless professionals, low handicappers and duffers alike. In fact, I have earned the tag of "The Swing Surgeon" from those whose swings I have carefully dissected, studied and reconstructed. I think that most of those swings have benefited from the "surgery"!

During my years of study of this fascinating game, I have worked constantly to understand the true fundamentals that govern an effective golf swing. This book is a detailed explanation of my philosophy of teaching golf. The purpose of this book is to provide golfers at all handicap levels with a complete analysis of the golf swing by taking a close look at what I now know are the basic swing fundamentals.

Most books on golf instruction are written to detail someone's new "secret" or "method" or "move." This book is different—it will not reveal any single new secret. Instead, it will key on the four basic fundamentals of the game (grip, stance, posture and alignment) upon which a sound golf swing must be built. From there, I progress logically through the execution of the swing and on to shotmaking, short-game play, strategy and all the other facets of this great game that you need to know about in order to enjoy it to the fullest.

Above everything else, solid fundamentals create a sound, repetitive swing that in turn produces good shots. It is my premise that the most helpful thing you can do for your game is to become aware of and practice good fundamentals. These, more than any series of magical moves or gimmicks, will add consistency to your swing and consistency to your shots. I promise you that the end result will be lower scores. Awareness and understanding of fundamentals is the most important "gimmick" you can use. Once you have finished reading this book, you will classify yourself as a "fundamentalist."

You might think that, given my emphasis, I might teach all my students to develop one identical swing pattern. In actuality, nothing is further from the truth. Part of the premise of this book is that golfers come in a variety of shapes and sizes, with different physical abilities. As such, they not only should but *must* have different swings. I also understand that there are differences in the mental and emotional capabilities from one golfer to the next. So I structure my philosophy with the understanding that although the laws and fundamentals are absolutes, not everyone can apply them to the exact letter.

While I accept that an inherent difference exists between each of us and our golf swings, I am still going to teach you the fundamentals. I would like to teach you to set up and swing soundly—as best your physical abilities allow—swing after swing and round after round. I believe in the following chain reaction:

Good Fundamentals = Good Setup = Good Swing = Good Results

My fundamental approach also accepts the fact that a certain player's physical abilities or disabilities may only allow him or her to hit one type of shot. All the same, if you are limited in your skills, you can learn how to plan for that particular shot, and then make that shot happen much more easily and consistently. In other words, grooving my fundamentals will enable you to hit a consistent hook or draw, if that is the maximum that your capabilities allow.

If you take the fundamental approach, you will have far fewer swing problems and greater consistency in the long run. You will learn to think over and be more careful with each and every shot.

Good fundamentals do not happen by accident. You have to work at them, shot after shot after shot. Take a close look at the typical PGA Tour professional's routine. If fundamentals were not important, he would not put such painstaking, meticulous effort into his setup. Jack Nicklaus is the best example of this approach.

I might also point out that Nicklaus, now a professional for a quarter of a century, still consults with his teacher, Jack Grout, for regular check-ups. If Nicklaus has a problem, it is usually one of the fundamentals that needs adjustment. A setup that is out of kilter means compensations in the swing, for Jack as well as for anyone else. You too should realize that it is all too easy to let a setup or swing fault creep into your game, no matter how diligent you may be. That is why I strongly recommend that you have a pro you trust periodically check what you are doing. Do this at the start of every season, at least.

I believe that golf is the ultimate sports challenge. You have no teammates to bail you out when you make a mistake. It is just you and the course and the elements. And you never really conquer golf. No matter how proficient you become, you can always perform better. The fascination, intrigue and challenge keep luring us back.

Throughout this book you will encounter my special expressions, words and phrases that I constantly use while teaching. Most are brief and to the point, others might seem downright corny. But they will work, just as they have with my students on the practice tee. If you do not believe me, just turn the page.

Part 1
Building Blocks for a Fundamental Golf Swing

1 What Makes a Good Swing Tick

Training the right muscles

Let's begin by looking at the actions that we all must make to produce that seemingly simple, yet often perplexing action known as the golf swing. This chapter will provide you with an overall analysis of the golf swing and the physical laws that govern it. This analysis will help you better understand the four setup fundamentals and how they affect your swing farther down the road.

Why do so many people find executing the golf swing such a difficult movement? The main reason is that for most of you, swinging a club requires using muscles you do not ordinarily call on in everyday life. If you are swinging with the wrong muscles, many of the moves you make will be incorrect.

Interaction of the various muscle groups is probably one of the most overlooked aspects of the golf swing. Very few instructors or books have adequately informed players of the interactions that occur in swinging the club. There is really no way you can set up in a fundamentally sound fashion if you are activating the wrong muscles. Knowing the right muscles enables you to set up to the ball in a way that prepares you to use these correct muscles and ignore those you do not want to use.

You need to know what the muscles do when you swing a club properly. First, unless muscles relax and contract, no physical activity can take place; and unless the proper muscles relax and contract, you cannot make a good golf swing. There are certain muscles that you must use and others that you must not. Simply put, good fundamentals "plug in" the good muscles and "unplug" the bad.

This is not a medical book, so I am not going to bog you down with scientific terms for these muscles. Instead, I will use the terms I have utilized in my everyday teaching. Let's evaluate what muscles you should be conscious of when you swing the club.

FINGER, HAND AND ARM MUSCLES. The first group of muscles to look at are the ones directly involved in holding the club. This is not the time for a detailed examination of what makes a good grip. Those secrets appear in chapter 3. For now, you simply need to know what muscles you should actively use.

Just about every book ever written and every lesson ever given states that the club should be held firmly in the last three fingers of the left hand, and I certainly agree. Applying pressure with these fingers activates the muscles needed to make the left arm the "power arm," as I like to call it. They activate the rear or "under" muscles of the arm as opposed to the arm's front muscles, which are controlled by the thumb and forefinger.

To prove this to yourself, extend your left arm in front of you and squeeze with your last three fingers only. You'll feel the muscles on the underside of your arm, from your wrist to your elbow, being activated or primed. Now if you squeeze these fingers a little tighter, you'll feel the "under" muscles being activated a little further up your arm, past the elbow. Before taking the club back, you must tighten the last three fingers of your left hand, so the left arm is firm—not stiff—with the "under" muscles primed and ready.

Firming up the last three fingers of the left hand to the degree needed for a good swing is difficult for most of us. Why? Because most of us are right-handed. We right-handers possess so much more power and strength in our right hand, arm and side than in our left, that we are apt to use the right side for anything that requires force or strength, including the golf swing.

When a "righty" plays right-handed (he actually plays from the *left* side of the ball) his left hand, arm and side must provide the power and control in the swing, not the right. A problem? Yes, but one you can solve. Here's how.

First, exercise your left hand and arm constantly. The stronger you can make them, the better they will govern your swing, while harnessing your right side. Make it a habit to squeeze a rubber ball or spring-loaded hand grip with your left hand.

Secondly, grip a club in your left hand and swing it one-handed. This excellent drill not only builds up strength in your left hand but really puts strain on the "under" muscles of your left forearm and the muscles of the left side and back. Practice this left-handed swing by slowly bringing the club up to the top of the backswing, then returning the club through the impact area and follow-through (see figure 1). When you repeat the swing, start from a stationary position, because merely sweeping the club back and forth will not build up or develop left-side muscles as efficiently. It is important that you swing the club from address through takeaway, then turn and extend your left arm and side all the way to the top of the backswing. Not only do you want to develop all the left side muscles mentioned, you also want to develop the sense or feel for a smooth, rhythmic takeaway and turn to the top of the backswing.

BACK MUSCLES. The back muscles are also a vital group in the performance of a sound golf swing. After years on the lesson tee, it is apparent to me that most golfers have no idea that their back muscles must be used both for proper technique and for power.

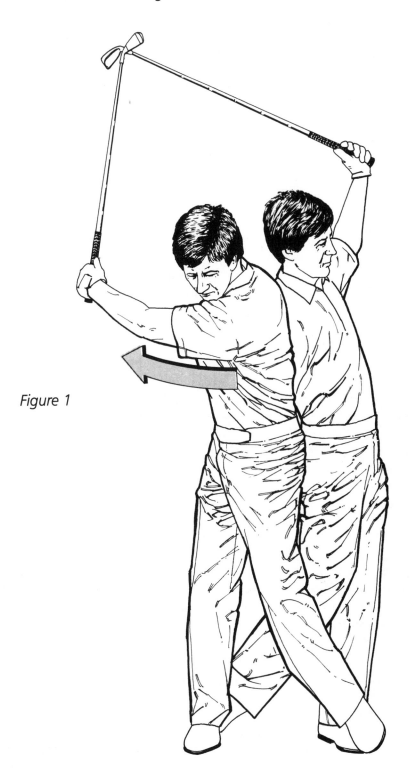

Figure 1

Try this experiment to get the feel of using precisely what muscles I'm telling you to use. Sit on the edge of a chair with your feet spread shoulder-width apart and your eyes looking ahead and slightly downward. Focus on an object as if you are looking at the ball and are about to swing at it (see figure 2). Next, place your hands against the front of your shoulders in crisscross fashion. Keeping your head still, twist from the waist as far as you can to the right, simulating the backswing turn. Then slowly twist back to the left, simulating the downswing turn and follow-through. You should feel the muscles of your back stretching on each side, all the way from your shoulder blades to your waist. Your left side stretches as you turn to the right, the right stretches as you turn to the left. This stretching of the back muscles is exactly the feeling you should get when you are making a golf swing.

Now let's examine *why* so many golfers have a problem using these groups of muscles—the underside of the left arm and virtually all of the back muscles.

There are basically two reasons. The first is that for most of us, our normal work and activities demand that we use what I call our "front" muscles. Daily actions, such as grabbing, lifting, holding, pushing and pulling, require that we use our forearm, bicep, chest and shoulder muscles extensively. When it comes time to swing a golf club, it is only natural to continue using the muscles that you use every day. These "front" muscles are more limber, loose, flexed and strong.

Meanwhile, orthopedic surgeons have warned us repeatedly that, because most of us do not use our back enough or do not use it properly when performing heavy work or lifting, we are extremely susceptible to backache and pain. Because we do not utilize these back muscles in our everyday activities and work, it is even harder to use them to swing a golf club.

The second reason golfers have problems using the correct muscles is that the swing is executed from a rather awkward position. Bent over at the waist and leaning toward the ball in front of you, you are in an unnatural postion. There is not much we do in life from a stooped-over position. When we sit at a table to eat, most of us sit in a fairly erect posture and lift the fork to our mouth. When we sit to read a newspaper or magazine, we hold it up so we can sit erect. Simply stated, human beings do most things from an erect or prone position. Bending over to hit a golf ball is bound to make us feel a little insecure.

I believe that this insecurity is the number one cause of poor fundamentals and poor swings. To set up properly, you must bend over at the waist; but by nature you are more comfortable and relaxed striving for erectness. However, standing erect puts you in poor position because it cues you to activate the "front" muscles mentioned earlier.

If you let these front muscles dominate the swing, you will succumb to the most common faults of beginners and high handicappers: raising the body during the backswing, letting your right side overpower your left in the down-

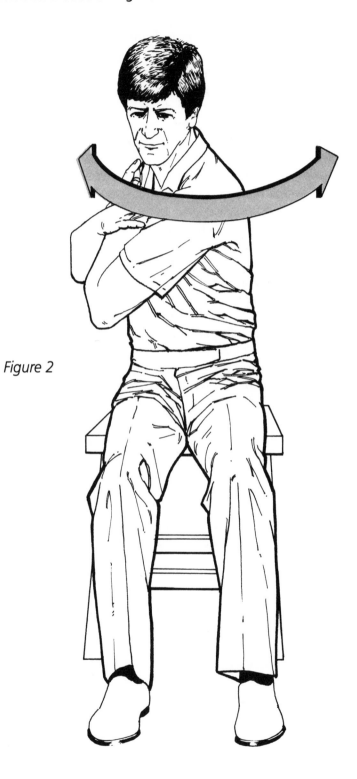

Figure 2

swing, cutting across the target line from outside in and creating a downswing path in which the clubhead descends steeply on the ball. The most common result of these flaws is that you impart a severe left-to-right spin on the ball. The shot you hoped to hit straight and true becomes the dreaded slice, bending into trouble on the right while costing you more distance than you can afford.

Other laws and forces affect the golf swing, as well. In a proper swing *centrifugal force*, the force that makes rotating bodies move away from their center of rotation, makes the clubhead move faster than the clubshaft, which moves faster than your hands, which move faster than your arms, which move faster than your shoulders, which move faster than your torso. The object of a fundamentally sound setup is to position your body at address so that you can produce maximum centrifugal force in the swing. I believe maximum force can be achieved only when the body is helping to swing the arms—not the reverse. The setup necessary to achieve this maximum centrifugal force asks us to bend over at the waist with our upper body leaning toward the ball and our knees flexed. Now we are primed and ready to use the back muscles for the coiling needed in the backswing turn. This twisting will feel tightest at your waist since your upper body is turning more fully than your lower body. When you start your downswing with a lateral move of the lower body to the left (as I will discuss in detail later), the uncoiling of the upper body starts your arms down much faster than your body itself is moving. And, of course, the club moves down even faster.

For every tiny bit that you're out of position, and thus using the wrong muscles, you're losing centrifugal force, which also means you're losing clubhead speed, yardage and consistency. That is why learning to set up perfectly is crucial.

Action-reaction is a second important principle in the golf swing. From my days in science class, I know that "for every action, there is an equal and opposite reaction." In golfing terms, this law means that when you turn to the right on the backswing, this move is automatically followed by a turn to the left on the follow-through.

In the golf swing I view the coiling-uncoiling of the body as action-reaction. When you coil properly on the backswing while adhering to sound fundamentals, you automatically trigger the reaction and the uncoil—and an automatic reaction and uncoiling on the downswing is what you want.

My purpose in mentioning these movements now is to give you an insight into the relevant laws of science so that when we get into a detailed analysis of the four fundamentals you will better understand why each of them is essential to enhancing your success ratio in swinging a golf club.

Let's now examine these fundamentals, which will help us overcome the problems of the golf swing I have described.

2 The Game's Four Fundamentals

Why your grip, stance, posture and alignment must be right

Now that you know the muscles you must activate in order to execute a fine golf swing, let's look at the fundamentals that put them into use.

My fundamental philosophy is based on the belief that there are four basics that must be correct before you draw the club back: grip, stance, posture and alignment. Each of these fundamentals is equally important; each is vitally inter-dependent upon the other three. In effect, these four fundamentals form a team, and your goal is to get this team to work as one. I can tell you from experience that neglecting any one of the fundamentals is enough to throw the entire mechanism, your golf swing, out of order. You will find yourself compen-sating in various ways during the swing itself, even though you may not even be aware of it. And trust me, these compensations almost never work well for long.

A good, fundamentally sound setup is the most vital step toward producing a repetitive swing and consistent results. The same setup produces the same results, time after time—even to the point where it becomes a little boring. Now, in general I do not want to be considered a boring person, but as a golfer, that's *exactly* what I want to be. Don't you dream of being a player who hits it straight down the middle off the tee, then nicely onto the middle of the green so consis-tently that your friends enviously say that your game must be boring? If you don't, you should.

To be boringly straight off the tee and to the green, you must begin by being so fundamentally consistent in setup after setup and shot after shot that your routine becomes routine. Your routine may take some time to develop, but gradually it will become habit, an exact pattern that is easy to perform time and time again. Once your routine becomes ingrained into your subconscious, your shotmaking will take on a new consistency.

Of course, you will always need to stay aware and to check periodically that you have not become careless or lazy or picked up a bad habit in your preswing procedure. After all, if Jack Nicklaus never slipped in his fundamentals, he would never need a tuneup from his longtime pro, Jack Grout. Yet even Nicklaus gets his checkups regularly.

Speaking of Nicklaus, I believe that he is by far the superior "fundamentalist" in professional golf, both past and present. His preshot routine and mannerisms are virtually identical, shot after shot, from the moment he approaches his ball.

Just picture Nicklaus standing by his bag with his hand on a club. He lifts the club out with his left hand on the grip and right hand on the clubhead and walks behind the ball to get a bird's-eye view of the shot he faces. He next locates a spot on the ground (in front of the ball and on the target line) which he uses as his aiming reference. Then he walks back to address the ball. With his weight on his right foot, he sets the club behind the ball, squaring the clubface to the interim spot he has selected. Next, Nicklaus plants his left foot and re-adjusts his right, checking that his feet are aligned parallel to his line of flight. Once he is confident that his body is aligned properly, he begins to waggle the club. Then comes the ever-present Nicklaus trademark of looking from ball to spot to target. Only when he feels set does he cock his head to the right, the movement that triggers his swing into motion.

I hope that at this point you are saying to yourself: "Yes, I can see Jack as clearly as if he is right in front of me." Nicklaus sets up exactly the same way every time. His procedure appears unconscious, as if it just happens, but it is a conscious process insofar as he is paying the necessary attention to make the fundamentals happen correctly. In tournament play, Nicklaus's procedure not only helps him prepare to swing correctly, but also, because he follows the same routine, reduces pressure he might otherwise sense.

Although we have focused on Jack Nicklaus's routine, the importance of a sound setup is reinforced by virtually all of the touring pros. Just watch them the next time you can get to a tournament, or on your television. You will notice that each player has his own specific routine.

Every tour pro realizes that the only way to achieve consistency in his shots is to swing consistently. And the only way he can achieve consistency in his swing is to be consistent in his setup, by being as fundamentally sound as he is physi-cally able. Now, if PGA Tour pros, aware of the need for good fundamentals, work so hard on them, that should tell amateur golfers like you something. You need to work just as hard on your own setup, if not harder.

Sure, you may say: "The pros play golf for a living, but I just want to have fun." I hear that from players all the time, but in most cases I believe that statement is a coverup. If you really played only for fun and had no interest in improving, you would not be reading this right now. So let's throw away any facade and acknowledge that you really do want to play to your highest potential.

Now that my pep talk is completed, I hope you'll make the commitment to work on your fundamentals of grip, stance, posture and alignment. Achieving these four basics to the best of your physical abilities will do more for your swing than any magic move, secret or technique in the swing itself.

Remember, *the setup predetermines the motion.* Make no mistake, a good setup, in and of itself, is the best preventive medicine for swing faults. Takeover of the swing with the right hand, coming over the top to start the downswing, outside-in swing path and many other flaws result from improper preswing fundamentals. It is amazing how close the correlations are between a player's setup and his swing. I can look at a player's setup and tell the person immediately how his or her shots will fly. For example, a player who sets up with his right side high, strong and dominant can do little but hit the ball with the right hand and arm controlling the downswing, making an outside-in action and a slice almost inevitable. This player can try to make corrections during the swing, but the compensations invariably fall far short of the desired result, and they cannot be applied consistently either.

Plainly put, you cannot make your body move in a way that is contrary to its nature. Just as water cannot turn uphill, a right-sided, dominant setup can only hinder the motion that will result in a good swing: taking the club straight back from the ball and slightly to the inside, with the left side dominant and the right side passive—all desirable elements, as we will see in chapter 5.

If you swing in this way, a change in your setup can weaken or soften the dominant right arm and side, allowing the proper takeaway and a good move to the top of the backswing. No forced or unnatural swing moves will be necessary.

My philosophy is one of fundamentalism in action. Set up properly, then work with the swing that emanates from that setup. Invariably, that swing will be both more effective and more consistent. Do not settle for a setup that forces you into poor swing technique.

So, amateurs of the world, admit that although you play golf for fun, you will have more fun, satisfaction, fulfillment and pride if you improve your game and play to your potential. Start by making sure you have a fundamentally sound setup. When you set up better every time, you will swing better every time. And your swing will last. Just look at all the senior professionals who are still playing super golf—Sam Snead, Gene Littler, Don January, Julius Boros, Art Wall. The list goes on and on. Each of these veterans still sets up and swings so consistently well that it is boring. Wouldn't you like to be just as "boring" for just as long? You can if you are as fundamentally sound as they are.

So let's now evaluate each of the four fundamentals in detail.

3 Building the Grip

A "power" left and a "passive" right

Because your hands are the only part of your body in direct contact with the club, your grip is ultimately responsible for putting the clubface squarely on the ball at impact—one very good reason to go that extra mile to perfect the grip. But before we actually study a fundamentally sound grip, let's examine what the hands and arms actually accomplish during a swing.

The hands and arms *rotate* as you execute your backswing. As the club moves back, this rotation helps the club to naturally swing open in relation to the target line. On the downswing, the arms rotate to the left, so that the club is then rotated back from an open position to a square position.

No matter how well you swing, if your grip is poor you will always have trouble making the clubface move squarely through impact. Assuming you have set yourself square to your target and intend to hit a relatively straight shot, at impact your clubface must be moving at right angles to your line of flight. Remember, too, that for the average player the club is approaching the ball at a speed of 100 miles per hour. With such velocity in the clubhead, gravity and centrifugal force substantially influence the movement of the club, so you must maintain a secure grip.

In order to play the game of golf well, you must play it with an extremely delicate sense of "feel." You will get the most vivid or sensitive "feel" of any object when it is in your fingers rather than your palms. Thus, your goal is to hold the club in the fingers of both hands.

The left hand (for right-handed players) is what I call golf's "power" hand. You should hold the club toward the end of your left-hand fingers. If you hold your hand open in front of you, you will notice that you have three joints on each finger. The first and second allow you to bend the finger, while the third (the lowest on each finger) is where the finger attaches to the palm. For the power left hand, you should hold the club between the second and third joints of the fingers, wrapping them around the club so that the fingertips brush up against the pad of the hand.

You should position your left hand so that the back of it faces the target. When you do this, you should also extend your thumb directly down the middle of the clubshaft. If it feels a bit more comfortable, extend it slightly to the right of the center of the grip. The choice is yours.

With the back of your left hand facing the target, your power hand is in a neutral position. The vast majority of you will find it simplest to return the clubface to a square position at impact when the back of the left hand is neutral or facing the target.

When you position your left hand as described, you will notice a small V formed by the inside of your thumb and forefinger. Quite a lot has been said about the Vs in the golf grip, to the point where they seem to take on more importance than the grip itself. Suffice it to say that the V on your left hand is merely a checkpoint. If the back of your left hand is facing the target with the thumb positioned down the right-center of the grip, your left-hand V will point to the right of your chin, toward the inside of your right shoulder.

Place the grip of the club under the pad of your hand so that if you hold your hand and the club out, your fingers underneath the club and the pad on top will give the club balance.

Incidentally, you should note at this point whether the grips on your clubs are the proper size for you. Your grips are the right size if, when you grasp the club in your left hand, the tips of the last three fingers just brush up against the pad of your left hand. If your fingernails curl under the pad or pinch into it, the grip is too thin for you. However, if the tips of your fingers do not reach the pad of your left hand, your grip is too thick.

Correctly fitting grips are essential, as they have a direct effect on the degree to which your hands and arms rotate during the swing. A grip that is too thick makes it difficult for you to rotate your arms, so that you tend to leave the clubface open at impact. An open clubface not only costs you distance, but imparts a left-to-right spin on the ball—a slice.

If the grip is too thin, a firm, solid hold on the club becomes more difficult. Consequently, the club is likely to turn in your hands. An overly thin grip can also cause you to turn your left hand more to the right, a "strong" position in which the back of that hand faces more toward the sky and causes an overrotation of the hands and arms through impact so that the clubface goes past square to closed at impact. The net result is a right-to-left spin on the ball, causing a hook.

If the back of your left hand points somewhat toward the ground, or if you place the club more in the palm instead of the fingers, your grip is in a "weak" position. The hands and arms cannot rotate enough to square up the clubface at impact, and the net result is usually a weak push or slice to the right. The weak left-hand position can also cause the club to turn or twist in your hands, weakening impact and causing loss of accuracy.

One last note on the left hand—the thumb should be placed naturally flat against the grip. This position allows important things to happen. First, the

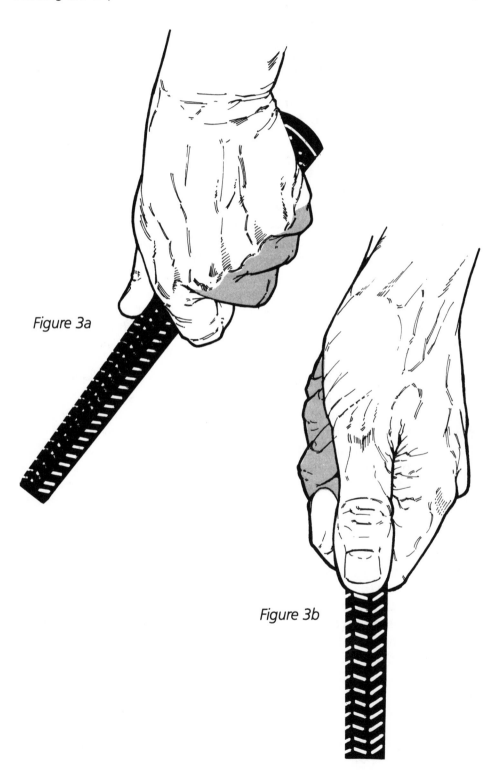

Figure 3a

Figure 3b

thumb acts as a support for the weight of the club at the top of the backswing, helping prevent you from overswinging. Second, the "long" thumb is a better visual guide to a square clubface: if your thumb points to the leading edge of the face, the clubface is square. Third, the thumb straight down the shaft (or a touch right of center) assures that the back of the left hand is aimed at the target. If you let your thumb slide to the right, the back of the left hand begins to creep dangerously close to an overly strong position prevalent among amateurs. This shift in position also encourages you to activate the biceps and shoulder muscles, the "front" muscles that you want to keep out of the swinging action, as I discussed in chapter 1.

This leads us to our last point concerning the left-hand grip—pressure points. The pressure on the grip should be applied by the *last three fingers* of the left hand, for three reasons: first, so that the club will not slip or turn at any point in the swing; second, so that when you change directions at the top of the backswing the force of action and reaction will not tear the fingers open and cause you to lose control of the club and force you to regrip on the downswing; and third, the pressure of the last three fingers assures that the muscles on the underside of your arm are activated. After all, you must use the correct muscles to make a high-quality swing. (For a look at the completed left-hand grip, see figures 3a and 3b.)

Now that we have the left hand properly positioned on the club, let's place the right hand correctly. Because your right-hand grip supplies the majority of the feel for each shot, the use of fingers is even more important than for the left hand. Since the left hand holds the club between the second and third joints, the right, for the sake of feel, should hold the club between the first and second joints. This placement puts the right hand in a more passive, no-power position.

Now, don't get me wrong, you will use the right hand during the swing. I simply want you to put it on the club in a more subdued fashion, where it will not overpower your left. The right hand's role should be that of a *helper*, not a hitter.

When you place your right hand on the club, you have the option of one of three grips. In any of these three grips, incidentally, the positioning of your left hand will remain the same. Since I believe that the hands should work together as a unit as closely as possible, I advocate the use of one of the two grips adopted by 99 percent of all players today: the Vardon, or overlapping, grip and the interlocking grip. Your choice should be based on three criteria: what feels most acceptable to you; what types of shots result when you try each grip; and the size of your hands. If you are not sure which grip to use, use the trial and error method, making sure that for either grip the positioning of the hands is fundamentally sound.

I really don't think that either the overlapping grip or the interlocking grip is superior; you should use the grip that fits your hands better. Let's discuss the interlock first. To form this grip, lift the index finger of your left hand off the grip

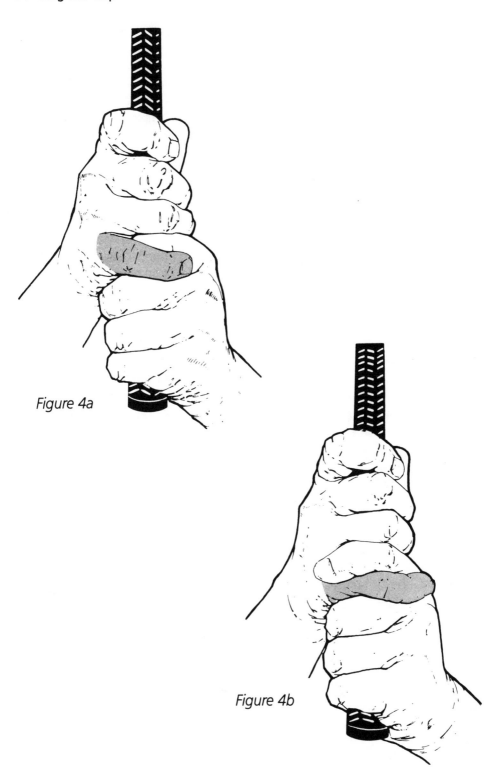

Figure 4a

Figure 4b

to allow the little finger of the right hand to slide in between the left-hand index and middle fingers. Then, interlock the little finger of your right hand with the index finger of your left, with both stretched out most fully. Lay your right-hand thumb over the left side of the grip. Your right-hand index finger should wrap around the grip and brush up against the thumb (see figures 4a and 4b).

The interlocking grip is probably the best grip to use if you have small hands or short fingers. If you use a "cadet" size golf glove, which means that your fingers are on the short side, I recommend that you use the interlocking grip. Your short fingers make it harder to wrap your fingers around the club, so the interlocking grip assures you of a more solid, firmer hold.

The Vardon, or overlapping, grip is very similar to the interlocking grip. The difference is that the little finger of your right hand is laid on top of the index finger of your left hand, overlapping it instead of interlocking with it. I believe this grip is better for players with large hands or long fingers, as it gets the right hand more on top of the left and off the grip itself. This grip puts your right hand in a position slightly more subservient to the left than in the interlocking grip.

As I said earlier, the V of your left hand is merely a checkpoint to ensure that your hand is positioned properly on the grip. The same holds true for your right-hand V. Whether you use the overlap or the interlock, the V formed by your right-hand thumb and forefinger should match the V of your left hand—that is, it should point to the inside of your right shoulder (see figure 5).

Finally, there is the oldest and simplest grip, the ten-finger or baseball grip. With this grip, you place your left and right hand on the club in the manner stated above, except that you place all ten fingers on the grip.

The ten-finger grip places the right hand and arm in a very powerful position, because unlike the overlap or the interlock, this grip places all the fingers of this hand on the shaft and makes most players very susceptible to holding the club in the palm of the right hand, encouraging a right-side dominant action as it activates the upper arm and shoulder muscles at address. Such dominance can cause all kinds of problems. If the right hand rotates over the left too much on the downswing, you will get a pull-hook. If your right hand moves through impact with no rotation, your hands hit the ball with the right palm up at impact; with the clubface thus open, the ball will start to the right, then slice even farther right.

I could go on and on about this grip, but I think you already understand why it is the least acceptable of the three grips. Why do I mention it? Well, it is a golf grip, one that has been used very successfully by certain players. Art Wall has made forty-one holes in one, and he is still playing successfully on the Senior Tour using the ten-finger grip. But the list of players successful with this grip is so small that its unacceptability cannot be doubted.

I will concede that the ten-finger grip can help certain players. If you know that your hands are relatively weak, you might be better off having all ten fingers on the club to help you to overcome the jarring effect of impact, which can dis-

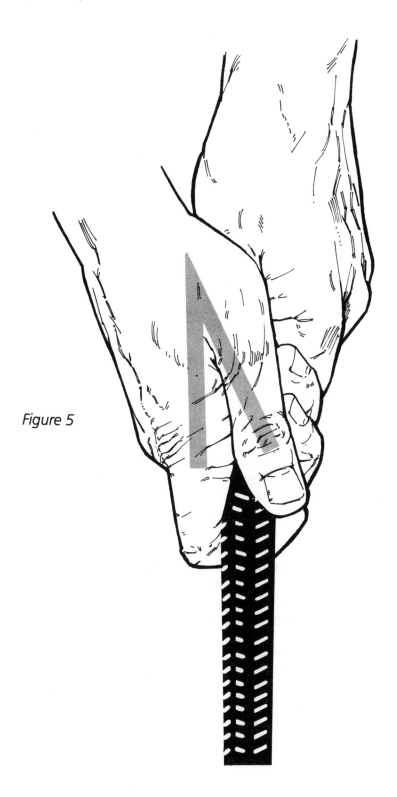

Figure 5

lodge the clubface from a square position if you do not have sufficient pressure on the club.

Now that you have your right hand on the club (hopefully in the overlapping or interlocking position), let's look at where you should apply pressure with that hand. I believe the middle and ring fingers should be the two major pressure points of the right hand. The thumb and index fingers should apply a little pressure to provide balance for the club at the top of the backswing. If there is no pressure to hold the club in place at the top of the backswing, the weight of the clubhead will cause it to drop, so that the grip lies against your right palm between your index finger and thumb. If that happens, you have lost control of the club.

In addition, the pad of the hand below your thumb should provide pressure from above the grip. If you squeeze too tightly with the fingers, especially the index finger, you will activate the upper right arm and shoulder muscles.

You have both hands in position. You are applying pressure at the proper points. How does this grip affect the position of your arms? Just as you have "power" and "passive" hands at address, so must you develop "power" and "passive" arms. More than anything else, the proper grip helps set up the correct arm positioning.

When both arms are extended at address, the left arm, the power arm, should be higher than the right. In other words, if you placed a club across your elbows so that it pointed along the target line, the shaft would also point a little bit upward.

The inside of your left elbow should point neither straight up nor horizontally, but at about one o'clock. Incidentally, allowing the inside of this elbow to face upward and to the right in this manner is contrary to Ben Hogan's analysis in *Five Lessons—The Modern Fundamentals of Golf,* where Hogan says that supple players can and should keep the insides of their elbows pointing straight up, while at the same time keeping the back of the left hand facing the target. But when the majority of players point the left elbow straight up, they find that the left hand rolls underneath, or turns too far left into a "weak" position.

Extend your left arm and turn the inside of the elbow straight up. If the back of your left hand rolls under or you have to strain to point it at the target, then you know your elbow must point toward two o'clock.

As for the right elbow, I agree with Hogan that it should point straight up. This position will cause your right arm to crook so that it is lower than the left, in a passive position. When you are set in this position, your left arm climbs over your right as you start the backswing. The left is the power, the leader, and the right is passive, the follower. The right arm will act like a piston—collapsing on the backswing and expanding on the downswing—moving at all times where the left arm forces it.

Now you can see how the proper grip influences other fundamentals of the swing. Let's sum up the key points to remember about your grip:

1. *Left (power) hand.* Grip the club between the second and third joints of the fingers, with fingertips brushing the thumb pad and back of hand facing the target. Grip pressure is in the last three fingers.

2. *Right (passive) hand.* Place grip between the first and second joints. Place the pad of the right thumb over the left thumb, with right palm facing left palm. Pressure in middle and index fingers.

3. Interlock or overlap the right hand little finger into or on top of the left index finger.

4. The Vs of both hands should point to the inside of the right shoulder.

5. Hands should be close together—the right hand covering the left thumb.

6. Practice this grip until it becomes second nature!

4 The Right Stance

"I must go to the ball, it does not come to me"

The second fundamental is the stance, for which you must perfect balance, weight distribution, width of the stance and ball placement.

Balance and Weight Distribution

Have you ever heard the advice that you should "sit on your heels," "lean back" or "imagine you're squatting on a bar stool" as you execute the swing? If you have studied golf instruction to a fair degree, you probably have, but I suggest you toss out these images immediately. They are 100 percent wrong, completely at odds with modern golf fundamentals. With today's modern equipment, your weight must be placed more forward at address, so that you are leaning into the ball rather than away from it. I like to use these expressions to remind myself of the proper weight distribution on my feet: "I must go to the ball—the ball does not come to me!" and "I must lean in the direction of the flow of the motion."

Common sense dictates this position. When you address the ball, you stand above it, with the ball lying on the ground. Your objective is to hit it from its spot on the ground in front of you, toward a target down the fairway. For the ball to move, you must apply force to it via all the movement and motion of your body, which is then transferred to the club. The ball is simply sitting there; it is not coming to you, so you must go to it. You must be leaning forward, out and over the ball, in order to properly and fully direct all of your motion and power to the ball while staying in good balance. I liken the position you should assume at address to standing on the edge of a pool, ready to dive in (see figure 6). To do this, your weight must be shifted forward, out and over the edge of the pool. In hitting the golf ball, your weight distribution should be the same: you must lean forward with your body out and over the ball, so you can move down to and through it at impact.

Another image you can use to remember proper weight distribution is that of a baseball batter. The ball is being delivered from the pitcher on a line that will pass in front of him. He must move to and through the ball in order to hit it. Picture a great major league hitter like George Brett or Don Mattingly. He leans forward, bent over at the waist, so he can step into and through the ball, delivering maximum power with good balance. The only difference is that baseball batters make this movement toward the ball on a more horizontal plane than the golfer does, simply because the ball is in the air rather than on the ground.

Consider the position a tennis player assumes while waiting to return a serve. The player bends over and leans forward. His weight is on the balls of his feet while his hands and arms are extended in front of him. Why does he assume this position? If you get up right now and try it yourself, you will see that from this position you can move with ease, speed and balance in any direction—right, left, forward, backward or at any angle.

Why is all this relevant to you? When you address the ball and swing, you turn to the right, then turn back to the ball and then finally turn to the left, up to the finish. You move in one direction on the backswing, then completely reverse yourself and move in the opposite direction. That reversal or shift must be made with good balance, and you can only have good balance if you properly set yourself in a fundamentally sound stance.

At address the weight on your feet must be forward, not back on your heels. When you bend over at the waist and lean forward, your weight should be on the balls of your feet. *You should feel light on your heels.* Of course, you do not want your weight completely on your toes, with your heels off the ground— then you would be leaning too far forward and literally falling into the ball at impact. Instead, you should feel that, at address, your weight is positioned where the flaps on your golf shoes are, or around the lower end of your shoelaces. This way, you feel free to lift your left heel off the ground on the backswing (if you must do so to achieve a full turn), and the right heel when you drive to and through the ball.

With your weight on the balls of your feet, you should have a nice flex in your knees. Notice that I said "flex" rather than "bend." If you bend your knees, you invariably lower your butt and move the weight back to the ankles or the heels—away from the ball—so that you feel your weight heavily on your heels. When you flex your knees, you ready yourself for the movement of the swing. The muscles in your feet, calves, thighs and on up through your body are taut and ready to move in harmony. To bend your knees is to put them in a position beyond the point where these muscles can remain firm, taut and ready to perform and respond.

The distribution of weight between your feet allows for some variation because of the differences in shotmaking situations, like club selection, lie, upslope or downslope. I discuss these variations in chapter 15. As a rule of thumb, however, for all full shots you should place a minimum of 50 percent of your weight on your left foot. For a driver, a 50-50 weight distribution between the feet is fine because you want the club to sweep through the ball on a level,

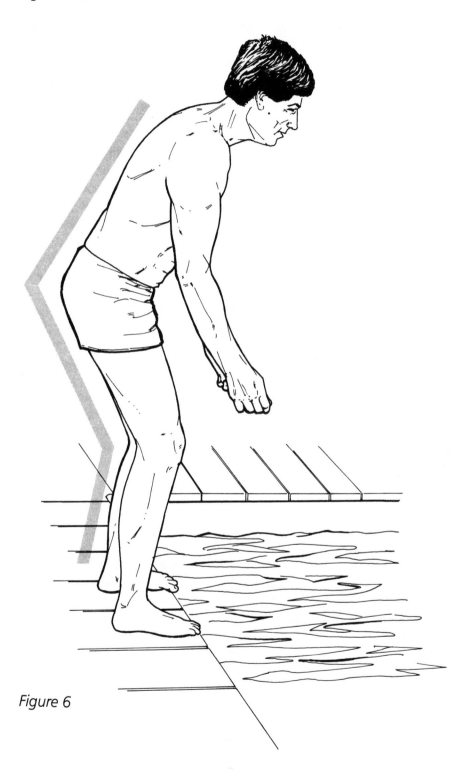

Figure 6

or even a slightly ascending, path. For a middle or short iron, however, you want the club to hit the ball with a slightly descending blow, so that you impart some backspin to the ball. In general with these clubs, you will find it is easier to do this when your weight is favoring your left side—say, 60 percent on your left foot and 40 percent on your right.

Width of Stance

An important facet of stance that determines your ability to keep your balance during the lateral movements that occur during the backswing and the follow-through is its width. If your feet are too close together, you will have difficulty making a full turn because as soon as you turn your weight onto the right foot, your hips and upper body weight would move beyond or outside your right foot, making you fall away from or off the ball. The same is true of the follow-through, when you move through the ball and onto your left side for the finish. If your left foot is too close to your right, you will fall back away from the ball to keep yourself from losing your balance to the left.

Just think how many times you have felt this loss of balance yourself, or how often you have observed other players stumbling in all directions, trying to avoid falling down. The reason is simply that their width of stance and weight distribution do not allow them to retain true balance throughout the motion of the swing.

What about the other side of the coin? If too narrow a stance can cause a problem, what about a stance that is too wide? Instead of falling over at the top of the backswing or in the follow-through, you will suffer from the opposite: you will immobilize your lower body, which in turn will reduce or eliminate the weight shift to the right leg on the backswing and the subsequent weight shift to the left side on the downswing.

So what is the *right* width? I believe in keeping the stance a touch narrower than many teachers advocate. For a 5-iron shot, the distance between the outside edges of your feet should be the same as the width of your shoulders (see figure 7 for proper widths of stance as well as ball positions). From the 5-iron to the driver, the longer the club the wider your stance should be, because as the club gets longer the arc of the swing naturally increases. Because there is more centrifugal force, the clubhead speed is faster, so you need a broader base to support and balance a longer, more powerful swing. For the driver, the inside edge of your left foot should be under the outside edge of your left shoulder, while the center of your right foot should be under the outside edge of your right shoulder.

The opposite is true from the 6-iron through the wedges. As the clubs get shorter, you should stand "narrower" to the ball because you make less of a backswing turn and generate less clubhead speed. With less movement taking place, you need less width between your feet.

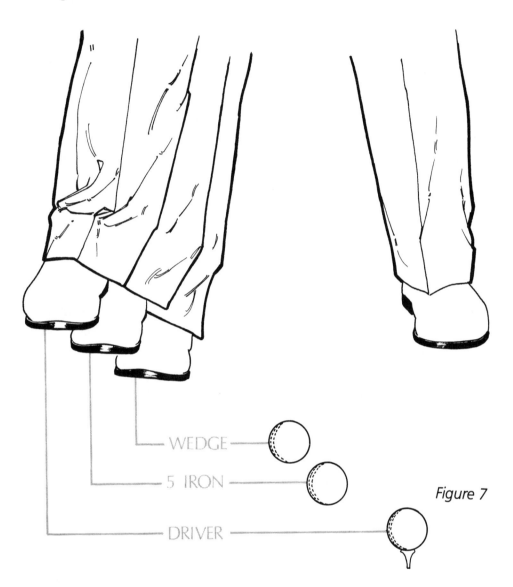

WEDGE

5 IRON

Figure 7

DRIVER

Ball Placement

Where you play the ball in your stance is vitally important. Ball position affects the shot's trajectory and direction, as well as the alignment of the clubface and body in relation to the target.

For the modern swing, there are two schools of thought regarding ball position. The first, which I believe in, teach and use, calls for the ball to be moved forward or back in the stance based on the club selected. With this system, you play shots with the wedges through the 7-iron from the exact center of your stance. As you move down through the longer clubs, you widen your stance as just described and move the ball to the left in your stance about one inch for each club. With this progression, you find that for a 2-iron shot the ball is opposite a spot just behind your left heel, for a 3-wood, the ball is opposite the inside of your left ankle, and for a driver the ball is opposite your left instep.

As the loft of your shot decreases, move the ball to the left in your stance. On shots that require less loft to get the ball airborne, you cannot descend on the ball as much. With my method, you move the ball toward the bottom of your swing arc for shots with the less-lofted iron clubs. The angle of attack at impact is shallower than with a wedge, so that the divot is also shallower, and the club sweeps the ball into the air. With the driver, you make contact as the clubhead is just beginning to go up after reaching its lowest point—a must for correct flight. This method of ball positioning also provides more consistent leg action and balance for all clubs.

The second approach to ball position is to play all shots from a point opposite the left heel or instep, and vary the width of your right foot to fit the length of the club. Many professionals and good amateurs use this method, which gives them the ability to hit the ball slightly higher and softer than they can with the system I advocate, an ability they need under testing tournament conditions, which include harder, faster greens.

But for the majority of golfers this method is not the best, because when the ball is placed forward for the middle irons through the wedges, most players are very susceptible to swaying, sliding or lunging into the ball to hit down on it. Most of us do not play and practice enough to maintain the agility and flexibility needed to drive the lower body to the left, keep the upper body back at the same time, and still hit down on the ball when it is placed in this position. With the ball placed up front for shorter shots, the average player opens himself up to excessive sway and movement, resulting in a high percentage of thin shots, skulls and directional problems, particularly the slice. So try my method instead.

The key to a good stance, then, is to keep your weight leaning forward into the ball—in the direction of the flow of motion. The proper width between your feet will allow maximum turn away from and then through the ball while in good balance. Correct ball placement will help produce the proper shot trajectory and direction.

5 How Posture Affects Your Swing

Why you shouldn't be totally comfortable

The third fundamental you must master in developing a solid golf swing is correct posture. Your posture at address is extremely important because it determines the plane on which you swing the club and helps you keep good balance. Your posture can also help you set your body in a position that aids proper timing during the swing.

One of the biggest misapprehensions players have about good posture is the assumption that if they are comfortable, their posture is automatically correct. This notion is false. I maintain that if you are comfortable over the ball, you *cannot* be in good posture. In fact, this misconception is one of many that are so common that I discuss them in detail in chapter 11.

The four steps to proper posture that I discuss below will help you place your body in a position in which virtually all your muscles from head to toe are primed, taut and ready to swing the club. Proper posture demands that you put yourself in a position over the ball that you rarely assume during everyday activities. I do not think you can ever be truly comfortable with it, by the very nature of the position and state of readiness your body must be in. Obtaining good posture means *getting accustomed to a relatively awkward position*.

Let's list the four steps you must take to put yourself in the proper posture:

1. *Straighten your spine.* Your spine should be firm but not absolutely stiff. Think of yourself as a soldier who is at "parade rest" rather than standing at attention.

2. *Bend over from the waist.* In plain English, you must stick your butt out slightly. Your spine should be tilted forward from the hips, with a little curvature at the base.

3. *Flex your knees.* Knees should be slightly flexed, but never severely bent.

4. *Extend your arms freely.* With the proper bend from the waist, you can simply let the arms hang from your shoulders.

Why do you need these steps?

First, at address and throughout the swing, you want to keep your upper body in as erect a position as possible, while still bending over at the waist. This straightening of your spine keeps your upper body from stooping over and your shoulders from curling up, habits you should avoid for a number of reasons.

When you swing the club, you must strive for maximum extension of your swing arc. That is, you should keep the club as far away from your body as the length of your straight left arm allows. The longer the distance the clubhead travels, the more clubhead speed you can develop. Remember that the distance the ball travels is determined by the clubhead's mass multiplied by its velocity squared (the golfer's application of the equation $e = mc^2$ that you may remember from your school days). So the speed at which the club moves is the overriding influence on distance. When you bend over at the waist, yet keep your upper body erect and you swing on a plane that is as extended and as upright as possible. That is the best way to build speed.

Since I've brought up the term "swing plane," let's examine how your posture affects it. The swing plane is the angle at which you swing your arms and the club through the backswing and downswing. You can best visualize the swing plane by imagining that the yoke of a wagon wheel is around your neck, with the bottom rim of the wheel at the point where the ball lies. The spokes of the wagon wheel represent your arms and the club, while the clubhead itself will be swung along the outside rim of the wheel.

At address, your arms should be just under the plane line formed by the spokes of the wagon wheel. During the backswing, your left arm should also be just underneath or brushing the plane line formed by the rim of the wheel, all the way to the top of the backswing. Once there, your arms and hands should remain just under this rim, which extends beyond your shoulders.

If your arm swing goes above the wheel's rim at any point during the swing, then your swing is more upright than it should be, given your height and posture. If your arm's swing is appreciably below that line during the swing, then you have a relatively flat swing.

Note that as you swing down, your arms should return the clubhead to the ball on a slightly flatter plane than it traveled back on. The club returns along a slightly flatter plane or arc because of the lower body's reversal of action when the club starts down from the top and your body bows slightly at the waist. This tilting drops your right side lower than your left, and thus you get the club returning to the ball on a flatter plane (see figure 8 for backswing and downswing planes).

Incidentally, when someone says your swing is too flat or too upright, never accept it as gospel without proof. If you do, you may start making unnecessary changes that will upset your "fundamentals" package. Be sure to check your swing plane for yourself. A simple way is to have a friend stand twenty feet or so directly behind you, using a clubshaft he holds before his eyes to represent the

Figure 8

plane running from the ball to your shoulders. Then he can tell you with certainty how closely your arm swing subscribes to your ideal plane.

Of course, the plane he measures is ideal only if you are bending forward from
the waist the correct degree. You need to bend over from the waist with your
spine relatively straight in order to establish the *relatively* upright swing plane—
relatively upright in relation to *your* stature—that I believe all golfers should
strive for.

A final key to determining the plane on which you should swing is your arm
length. Two players might be of the same height, but if their arms are of different length they should swing on different planes. The longer the player's arms,
the greater the extension or angle of his arms and the flatter his swing must be.

When your upper body is bent over at the waist with the spine erect, it is in a
position that allows it to twist or coil against your lower body. You can create
what I call "upper body-lower body separation." This separation takes place at
the waist. You have obtained separation when, during the backswing, your
shoulders and upper torso twist or coil against the hips, which do not turn as
much. However, at the start of the downswing, your lower body, legs and hips
begin to uncoil while the upper body still lags behind—the action-reaction discussed in chapter 1. Action-reaction can only take place if there is separation,
and you can only have separation if you straighten your spine and bend over at
the waist with your butt out.

The third step to perfecting your posture is to flex your knees. I stress the word
"flex" here rather than "bend." To me, "flex" implies just cracking the knees a
touch. In no way do I want them to be bent at a severe angle. Bending the knees
automatically causes your upper body to fall back away from the ball and, in
turn, causes your weight to move back toward your heels, which you know from
the previous chapter is undesirable.

In order to keep your upper body out and over the ball in good balance, you
need to keep your leg muscles firm and taut, which you can achieve only by
slightly flexing or cracking your knees. When you do this, the muscles of the
upper and lower legs are primed and ready, whereas if your legs are bent too
much, your leg muscles will relax; they cannot be kept firm or taut enough to
provide the precise leg action and balance that a good swing demands.

The fourth step toward good posture is to extend your arms comfortably. If
you have properly performed the previous steps and have your upper body tilted
out and over the ball, extension of the arms really amounts to letting them just
hang from your shoulders. Your hands should be positioned so that if you draw
a line straight up from your hands, it extends to a point on your face between
your nose and your chin. If the line is inside your chin, your hands are too close
to your body. If the line points outside your nose, to your forehead or beyond,
you are reaching too far for the ball.

Another good way to judge whether you are extending or reaching too much
(a more common fault than keeping the arms too close to the body) is to notice

Figure 9

whether you feel any pulling between your shoulder blades. If so, you have extended too far and need to get your hands closer to you.

It is vitally important to find your proper arm extension. If you reach too much, you will be forced to bend over too much, and you will have problems maintaining your balance during the swing. You will also set up and swing the club on a flat plane. If you do not extend enough, your swing will be too upright or will come across your body, since a lack of arm extension means you stand too close to the ball, with your body in the way of an on-plane backswing.

How should the arms be positioned in order for them to work properly? Assuming that you want to hit the ball straight, or possibly with a little draw, you *must* set up with your left arm in a comfortably extended power position and your right arm in a slightly folded passive position. That is, your left forearm should be higher than your right one.

Remember that the left arm is your power arm, and nearly an extension of the clubshaft (see figure 9). It must remain firm and extended throughout the swing. The arc described by the club during the swing is nearly a perfect circle, and the left arm acts as its radius. It is the guide that brings the club squarely back to the ball at impact, provided there has been no lateral or vertical body movement to affect the delivery of the clubface. Conversely, the right arm must be the passive arm, the follower. The left arm, in extending away and around during the backswing, must force the right arm to collapse. For the right to collapse naturally while offering no resistance, it must be lower than the left at address so that the left can climb over it on the takeaway.

The biggest problem most of us face is that, being naturally right-handed, we tend to address the ball with the right arm in a dominant position—higher than the left and, in most cases, stiff instead of flexed, even to the point of being locked. From this position, you are almost forced to lift the club up and outside the line of flight, producing an outside-in swing that produces a glancing blow and a slice.

Good posture—especially being very careful to keep your left arm in the power position—is the best way to get the ball to fly in a consistent pattern. Later on, when we discuss shotmaking in chapter 13, you will learn how and when to vary your posture slightly in order to hit different types of shots. But if you want to hit the ball the same way time after time, you must set up to the ball the same way time after time. Remember, the setup predetermines the motion.

6 Perfect Alignment

Keep the lines ''parallel left''

Now the final step of our setup fundamentals—aligning your body and the clubface correctly. If you have developed an excellent grip, stance and posture, you are in great shape to make a swing that will produce shots that soar for good distance with a nice trajectory. But unless you have aimed your body and the club properly in relation to your target, the ball will not go where you intend it to.

Let's begin our examination by looking at ''square'' alignment—setting up the shoulders, hips, knees and feet so that lines across them would point exactly parallel to a line pointing to the target. Incidentally, I prefer to use the term ''alignment'' rather than ''stance,'' because ''stance'' implies that the only part of your body involved in alignment is your feet. Proper alignment of your knees, hips and shoulders is equally important.

The first thing that I ask my students when I'm giving a lesson is, ''What are you aiming at?'' The only way I can determine whether your fundamentals are in order is to know on what line you want to hit the ball. And I must know whether you intend to hit a straight shot. The only way that anyone can judge whether your setup is square, open or closed, and understand the flight pattern of your shots, is for you to have a definite target for every shot you hit.

This is especially important to remember when you are practicing. If you are not target-oriented during practice, you will never get accurate and reliable feedback on your setup, flight pattern and the final result of the shot. This major oversight is why so many golfers become what I call ''range players.'' These players can hit decently struck shots on the practice tee all day long, but they have little or no regard for the direction of their shots. One flies down the middle. One tails to the right. The next shot goes more to the left. But the range player is satisfied with them all, as long as his shots stay within the confines of the range or a section of it.

The problems begin once the range player steps out on the course. To his dismay, he finds that shots that seemed acceptable are instead heading into the right woods, the left trap, even out of bounds. He may have hit the ball with the same flight pattern and distance as he did in practice, but a shot that looked fine in the wide open spaces of the driving range looks a lot worse as it flies into the woods or into a greenside trap. If you want to be more consistent in direction, you must be conscious of alignment, whether you are in the midst of a practice session or an important match.

The first step to good alignment is to determine the line of flight you want the ball to travel on. Do this by mentally drawing a straight line from your ball to the spot where you want the ball to end up (assuming you want to hit a straight shot). All references to your alignment as "square," "open" or "closed" are relative to this line of flight.

In a setup that is square to the target, your clubface should be perpendicular to your line of flight, and lines across your toes, knees, hips and shoulders should be *parallel left* to your line of flight (see figure 10).

Before I describe a sure-fire routine to help you line up more consistently, with good posture, I want to tell you a little story about an incident that made me realize just how critical alignment is to your shotmaking.

In 1967, my freshman year in college, I played in a number of college matches at the Country Club of New Bedford, Massachusetts. My "problem" hole was the 18th. It was an uphill par 4, 420 yards. Off the tee, the hole turned a little left; from the landing area it gently curved back to the right and up to an elevated green.

The tee was set back in some large oak and elm trees. On the right side the trees only went out about 60 yards; on the left they lined the fairway for at least the distance of a good drive. For the first 150 yards in particular, these trees were in close and pretty confining.

The first half-dozen times I played the hole, my drive always ended up in the right rough, a deep, thick, moist rough, the kind from which you have to chop an 8- or 9-iron out about 100 yards. There was no way to reach the green from it. Yet every shot I hit into that rough was a well-hit drive in terms of flight pattern, trajectory and distance. I would hit a good-feeling, good-looking drive, yet always wind up in that right rough!

Finally, and partly by accident, I figured out the reason for my problem. While waiting to tee off on the 18th, I dropped a ball and chipped toward the rear of the tee. I walked back to pick up my ball, turned around and looked back the long, narrow tee and up the fairway.

First, I noticed that the tee pointed into the right rough, exactly where I hit my drive every time. With this revelation, I picked up my driver and stood on the tee, lined up the same way I always had, put the club on the ground across my toes, then stepped back behind the ball to check my alignment. Sure enough, the line extending across my toes pointed up the right edge of the fairway. The line of flight of the ball itself, parallel to my toe-line and to the *right* of it, was about 15 yards into the rough. (See figure 11.)

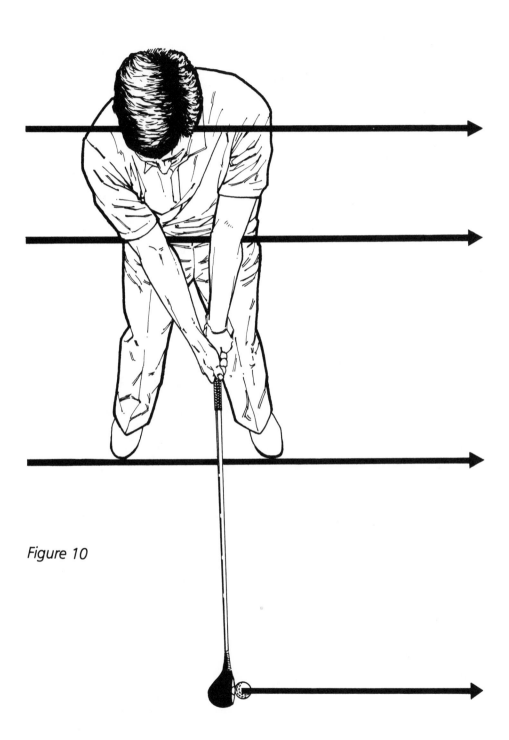

Figure 10

Figure 11

Next, I moved the club on the ground so that it pointed up the left side of the fairway. Now the target line over which the ball would fly was up the middle of the fairway. I stood back up to the ball, toes even with the club, picked the club up and addressed the ball. Then I looked up the fairway—and the second problem jumped out at me.

When my body was set up parallel left of my line of flight, which was up the middle, my body was lined up very close to the giant oaks and elms that lined the left side of the fairway. When I addressed the ball and looked up, the presence of these giant trees automatically forced me to aim to the right—something further encouraged by the alignment of the tee toward the right rough.

To recap: first, you can never trust the alignment of the tee itself. Just think now about your home course. I'll bet that more than one tee points into the rough, woods or even out of bounds. The second problem is a visual one. Trees, fences, buildings or whatever else is in close to one side of the tee and fairway will definitely influence your visual perception when you are over the ball. They can and will induce you to aim a little more to the other side—and far away from the fairway as well.

Now that these problems have been exposed, how do we correct them? In my particular case on the 18th tee, I walked away from and back up to the ball four or five more times, and each time I looked up, the tee was pointing me to the right. If I aligned properly, I saw my body pointing toward the trees, and my mind naturally told me to move to the right to avoid them. So I realized that I had to

Figure 12

devise a way of getting over the ball so that I would not have to look up to see if my body alignment was parallel to my target line—because those obstacles might cause me to change.

After some thought, the answer came to me. I squatted behind the ball and lined up the name so that as the ball rested on its tee the name pointed down the fairway to exactly where I wanted the ball to end up. After visualizing the shot, I stepped up to the ball in such a way that an imaginary line across my toes was exactly parallel to the name on the ball (see figure 12). I also made sure that my clubface was perpendicular to the name. My alignment had to be square. I would not even have to look up and get intimidated by those trees. Instead, I would remember the picture of the hole and the shot I intended, and I would swing freely.

To this day I rarely look at the target after I address the ball. There is another advantage to this habit. Every time you look up and see rough, traps, woods, lakes or out of bounds, you see places where you do not want the ball to end up, reinforcing negative thoughts, fear and panic. Glancing up makes you susceptible to making changes in your alignment as you steer yourself away from what you perceive as trouble.

Next time you play, watch and see how your playing partners make adjustments after they have planted themselves. I have found that most of the time, players align correctly the first time they step up to the ball. Looking up definitely tends to change your visual perception and alter your setup.

If you've thought ahead, you might be saying to yourself, "Aiming the name of the ball on the tee is a good idea, but what do I do when the ball is in the rough or on the fairway, so I can't move it to point the name?" My answer is to pick some discernible spot immediately in front of the ball—no more than two feet in front of it—that is directly on the line of flight. When you get over the ball, draw an imaginary line from the ball to this spot and carefully align the leading edge of the clubface perpendicular to this line. (See figure 13.) Also, position your feet, knees, hips and shoulders parallel to your aiming line. Incidentally, Jack Nicklaus is the most famous player using this method to better ensure proper alignment.

Now that you understand the importance of alignment, what might still give you trouble? When you stand behind the ball and look down the fairway to determine your line of flight, both of your eyes are facing the target. When you are bent over the ball and want to look down the fairway at your target, your eyes are to the left of the ball, at a slight angle to your line of flight. Therefore, when you roll or twist your head to look from the ball to the target and back, your mind sees a slightly curved or elliptical line. Because you are standing to the left of the ball, and your field of vision (in turning to the target) moves from right to left, this line is curved to the right.

If you are right-eye dominant, this curve is even greater, because you have to turn your head more to the left in order for your dominant eye to focus in on the

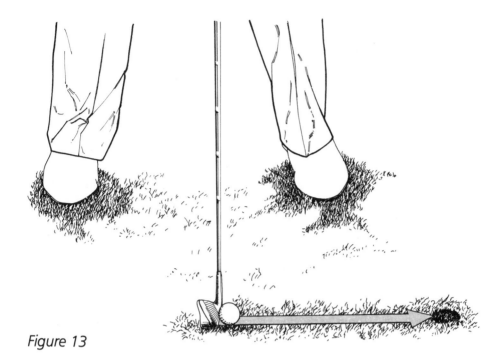

Figure 13

target. This curve accounts for the fact that 95 percent of all golfers line up to the *right* of their target.

In addition, a vast number of golfers believe that they are lining up correctly when a line across their toes points directly where they want the shot to finish, instead of pointing "parallel left" as described earlier. One final example: when you shoot a rifle, do you aim yourself or the gun at the target? You aim the gun, aligning your body to the left. Golf is the same. Now you know that this is "right" for sure—way to the right of the target, that is!

Using the name or a spot in front of the ball for alignment on every full shot overcomes these visual misconceptions. While you are actually addressing the ball, focus on the perception you had of the target from behind the ball, and do not look up before swinging.

My experience on the lesson tee also tells me that it is easier to line up the clubface than it is to line up your feet and body. Therefore, if you get the clubface square and then place your body perpendicular to the clubface, you will greatly increase your chances of obtaining square alignment.

Your clubface is square when its lower or leading edge is perpendicular to the line of flight. Your body is square when your eyes, shoulders, hips, knees and feet are parallel left of the line of flight. Your eyes should be parallel to the line of flight because if you tilt your head to the right, as many golfers do, your mental picture of the line of flight will also be closed or pushed to the right, triggering in your mind a muscle adjustment that makes you pull or hook the ball

back to the target. Conversely, if your head is tilted to the left, your mind perceives the line of flight as being open to the left, inducing you to adjust your
swing so that you push or slice the ball back to the right.

The angle at which your eyes are set definitely affects the way you visualize
your shot. If you want to hit consistently accurate shots, you must start with your
eye-line parallel to your line of flight.

Getting back to the shoulders, hips, knees and feet, let's analyze why we want
them to start from the same point of reference. To get a proper and complete
coil of the upper body against the lower body in the backswing, your shoulders,
hips and feet must start at the same place if they are to move proportionately. A
good shoulder-turn will be about 90 degrees to the right on the backswing,
while a proper hip-turn will be about half as much—45 degrees. The upper
body and lower body must start from the same position relative to the target
line.

If your alignment is not square, it is either open or closed. An open alignment,
in which the body is aligned left, tends to cause the ball to be pushed or sliced
to the right. Notice the opposite effect—body aligned left, ball flies right. This
occurs because the upper body, since it is starting from farther to the left, never
turns far enough to get behind the ball at the top of the backswing. Thus, when
the upper body moves into the downswing, it gets too far ahead of the ball at
impact. The result is a weak position at impact, a sharply downward attack on
the ball and an outside-in swing path, giving the ball a clockwise spin so that it
sails away to the right.

The closed alignment position finds the shoulders, hips and feet aiming to the
right of the target. The result of this setup is that the club approaches the ball
from a flatter and more inside-the-line angle of attack. At the top of the swing,
the body is farther behind the ball than it needs to be because it was turned farther to the right at address. From this alignment the club will usually be released
fully before impact, so that the clubface is closed as it makes contact. Thus, the
counterclockwise spin and the right-to-left ball flight. (See figures 14 and 15 for
open and closed alignments.)

If you align too much to the right or left the ball will usually not curve in the
expected direction to the degree that you have visualized. When good players
need to hook or slice a shot, they alter their setup without changing their grip
or swing. Trial and error tells them how open or closed their alignment should
be to obtain the desired hook or slice. Still, in most cases even experienced,
talented players get too little or too much "bend."

This point leads us back to our fundamental approach. To hit a relatively
straight ball, you must set up square to the target line. The shortest distance
between two points is a straight line, and a square setup will improve your
chances of hitting your ball right on that straight line. The more adept you

Figure 14

Figure 15

become at aligning squarely, the less often you will need to worry about setting up to hit hooks and slices.

Now we have the groundwork for the swing in place. Let's go ahead and begin swinging the club!

Part 2
The Swing: Sound Mechanics in Fluid Motion

7 Start with a Perfect Takeaway

Put the clubhead in the "mitt"

Now that we have fully covered the four preswing fundamentals, let's look at what they are intended to promote—a sound, functional golf swing. Just as there were four preswing fundamentals to study, so the swing itself divides into four segments that help you to assimilate the mechanics correctly.

The first segment of the swing, as you might guess, is the takeaway. Once you have learned to move the clubhead away from the ball correctly, you can "add on" each of the remaining swing segments—the move to the top, the crucial transition into the downswing and finally impact and follow-through. It will take a little time, patience and practice, but soon you will be able to mold the four swing segments into a well-timed, smoothly repetitive action. It helps immensely, though, to break the swing down first into easily understandable segments so that you learn to execute the mechanics as consistently as possible.

Before we start, let me stress one more important point. Everything that is stated here regarding the swing is designed to deliver maximum results for every player. My fundamental approach acknowledges that you may not be able to perform every movement of the swing as efficiently as the next player. Thus, you may have to alter or adjust your performance of these principles slightly, in order to fit your abilities. That adjustment is a matter of trial and error that every golfer must work out for himself or herself, and it is the main reason that no two swings end up being identical.

A smooth takeaway is what gets the whole golf swing into motion. Move the club away from the ball slowly, smoothly and on the correct plane for your body, and you are one step closer to owning a fine golf swing.

I believe that the swing should be initiated in what I term the "one-piece" takeaway. However, the term "one-piece" has been interpreted in different ways. Some people think that "one-piece" refers to a takeaway dominated by the hands; others, the arms; still others, the left arm and shoulder.

I do not agree with these definitions. I define a one-piece takeaway as one in which the clubhead's movement is begun by the turning of your torso and your shoulders. Meanwhile, the club is merely held passively in your hands. *By this I mean that your hands and arms are put into motion by your upper body.* This motion of your torso and shoulders carries down to your hips, legs and feet. I like to think of this takeaway in terms of the analogy, "Does the tail wag the dog or does the dog wag the tail?" In this type of takeaway, the dog is definitely wagging the tail—your body is initiating the backswing.

In the passive or one-piece takeaway, the butt end of the club should remain pointing to your breastbone or shirt placket *for the first two feet that the clubhead moves.* This "connection" of the chest with the movement of the clubshaft ensures that there will be no wrist break or flippiness, which tends to put the club into motion too quickly, leaving the body behind. When the clubshaft moves away from the center of the body at the start, the body will rarely be able to turn enough to catch up. The one-piece takeaway, initiated by your torso, is essential to a better backswing turn because it keeps the body moving the clubhead. Otherwise you may start what I call a "false" backswing by flicking or breaking your wrists and picking the club up. By turning your hips and shoulders, you produce a takeaway that gradually brings the clubhead inside the target line as well as away from the ball.

In my teaching, I've developed a gimmick, if you will, that I think provides a sharp mental picture of how to execute the takeaway. I tell my students to try to "put their clubhead into a catcher's mitt."

Imagine as you address your shot that there is a baseball catcher in full gear directly behind your line of flight, with his glove outstretched as if ready to catch the pitcher's delivery (see figure 16). Your one-piece takeaway should have you turning your entire upper body, so that your arms, hands and the club are extended straight back, putting the clubhead into the catcher's mitt.

Think of the catcher's mitt as being held as a target over the low-inside corner of the "plate"—that is, about two feet behind you and one foot above the ground. Up to the point that you have placed the clubhead in the mitt, you should make no conscious or forceful movement of your hands, wrists or arms in swinging the club away. Your club, hands and arms should move because your body *made* them move.

You can achieve the true one-piece takeaway by turning your hips and shoulders around your spine, setting the arms and club in motion. Another way to picture this "inside-out" chain of motion is by considering a wagon wheel. All movement begins at the center, the hub. The instant the hub moves, the farthest extremity of the outer rim moves. And depending on the length of the spokes, that outer rim moves much farther and much faster than the hub. The takeaway is exactly the same, except that your torso acts as the hub and the clubhead as the outer rim of the wheel.

A great many of today's professionals are teaching golfers merely to take the club away from the ball with their arms, claiming that everything else will follow naturally. I disagree with this advice because I believe that the body's extremi-

Figure 16

ties, in this case the arms, cannot effectively move the greater mass of the body. Does the tail wag the dog or does the dog wag the tail? We know that the dog should wag tail. I believe that the turning movement of the hips and shoulders sets the arms in motion.

I keep stressing the role of the hips during the takeaway because I believe that they are the key factor. Here is an exercise that proves the dominance of the hips over the hands, the arms and even the shoulders. Stand erect. Turn your shoulders to the right, taking notice of how far you can turn your shoulders before your hips begin to respond and move. The more supple you are, the longer it takes for your hips to respond. Leaving your shoulders immobile or neutral, turn your hips to the right, while watching for the corresponding movement of your shoulders. If you are like most golfers, you will notice that your shoulders respond to your hip movement much faster than your hips respond to your shoulder movement. In fact, they respond almost immediately. Notice that in most cases even a slight twitch of your hips will initiate a response from your shoulders.

The examples above clearly show why a one-piece takeaway initiated by a turning of the hips and followed by the shoulders is the very best way to set the swing in motion. Because you use the largest parts of your body to start the swing, you are most likely to be consistent. You will also find that this takeaway method is the best for maintaining good tempo.

How do the hands and the clubhead move during the takeaway? When you address the ball, your right hand should be even with the ball, a position that places your left hand slightly ahead of it. Your left arm is then in a position that is more or less an extension of the club, so that the club and hands are in a good position for a takeaway with the club "leading" the hands going back.

Your left hand should be on the club so that the wrist is aligned straight down the shaft. The wrist should not be arched toward the target (convex) or cupped away from it (concave) at all. A good checkpoint for your takeaway is the position your left wrist—at address it should not change during the takeaway (nor through the entire backswing and downswing—more on that later). If the angle of the back of the left wrist at address changes from its flat or square position during the takeaway, your swing has to be "wristy" or "handsy." You will either be lifting the club above the correct plane or flicking it inside on too flat a plane. Either of these moves will have to be corrected somewhere else in the swing. Most players try to make corrections when their hands are about chest-high in the backswing. Usually this move is unsuccessful—the chances of the wrists moving back to where the back of the wrist is a straight line with the club on the correct plane are slim.

Putting the clubhead "in the mitt" is an excellent way of assuring yourself of making a one-piece takeaway with passive use of the arms and hands. It is especially helpful in guaranteeing that the straight line at the back of your left wrist at address does not change.

Once you have put the clubhead in the mitt, you have taken the club back about two feet and the arms are now ready to take over some of the activity. So now let's see what you must do to make a complete, sound backswing.

8 Build Control into Your Backswing

"You can't cheat Mother Nature"

What should you want to accomplish as you swing the club up to the top? You want to execute a backswing in which your club moves on a consistent and correct plane so that you obtain the proper angle of attack during the downswing and an on-target swing path and face angle at impact. And of course you want to develop as much coil as possible while keeping control of the club. Your move to the top should be on-plane, balanced and controlled.

Remember that, to a great extent, your posture at address determines your backswing plane. Every golfer should try to swing on as upright a plane as possible, so at address keep your spine tilted forward from the waist and try to keep it that way throughout the swing. This posture naturally allows your shoulders to turn on a more tilted plane, letting you put the clubhead in the "mitt" on the takeaway. Then you continue on by swinging the club up around your neck, not your chest.

The reason you need to swing back on an upright plane is simple—your center of gravity is located in the nape of your neck. The neck is the hub of the tilted wagon wheel that the arc of your swing resembles. In order to create maximum centrifugal force, you must swing the club around your center of balance, that is around your neck.

My teaching experience has revealed that the vast majority of amateurs make their backswings on too flat a plane, revolving around their chest or shoulders. There are usually two reasons for this. The first is poor upper body posture at address, with the spine hunched or bent over instead of being straight but tilted, poor posture causes the player to swing the club too much around him. Second, many players take away the club so that it moves immediately to the inside, leading to a flat plane all the way to the top.

Most golfers have the impression that to make a good swing, they must take the clubhead away on a path that is inside the target line and then return it from inside the target line. They are right on both counts, but their perception of the degree to which the clubhead moves inside the target line is exaggerated. As a result, many players overdo it and swing their arms on a plane that is much flatter than the plane dictated by the tilt of their shoulders at address. They are then in a position from which they can generate much less power at impact than if they kept the club on-plane. You can develop substantially more power from a steeper angle of attack than most amateurs make.

Once you have completed your takeaway by putting the club into the mitt, your body should continue to turn in such a way that your hands and arms raise or swing the club more up than around. Here is an image that will help you. Picture a tree that is one foot wide directly behind the aforementioned "mitt." Then try to make your clubhead travel straight up the trunk of the tree.

Remember that you must keep both your hips and shoulders turning after you have completed the takeaway. Even golfers who execute a solid takeaway tend to let their arms and hands lift the club to the top on their own. Your arms and the club should never move in the backswing without the hips and shoulders initiating the movement. Think of it this way: in order to retain control of the club in the backswing, your arms and club must not move after the shoulders and hips stop turning.

All right. You are continuing your backswing with your body moving your arms so that the clubhead is moving back "up the tree trunk." A question you might logically ask at this point is, "How much backswing is right for me?" Well, the answer to this question is different for every player, because every player is capable of making a different degree of hip and shoulder turn. Some supple players can swing the club so far back that the shaft goes beyond being parallel to the ground while they still retain firm control of the club. Others should settle for swinging the club back so that it does not quite reach parallel. Still others who are less flexible would be better off swinging the club so that the shaft is only a little past being perpendicular to the ground—if that is the limit at which they can stay in control. As I like to say with regard to how far you swing the club back, "You can't cheat Mother Nature." You may *think* that you are when you twist the club around your neck by letting your left arm break down completely. But the truth will become evident very shortly thereafter—at impact.

Now is a good time to mention my preferences concerning the use of your legs and feet as you work the club up to the top. As you already know, the turning of your torso will exert some pressure on your lower body to turn as well. Your left knee will be pulled in toward the ball, and your left foot will rotate over to its inside edge as your weight shifts onto your right foot.

Your left heel may lift slightly off the ground as well, although I prefer that you keep the inside of your left foot on the ground if possible. If you let it rise, there is always a chance that you will put it down in a different spot, a mistake that can contribute to off-center hits. So let your left heel roll inward rather than lift off the ground on the backswing, even if the total length of your backswing winds up being a little less.

This might be hard to believe, but one of the biggest causes of players over-swinging is their failure to turn their shoulders and hips *enough*. These players stop turning too soon (or perhaps make a relatively small turn due to a lack of suppleness), but then try to make the club keep going, leading to either of two flaws: 1) a reverse tilt in which your weight actually shifts back from your right foot to your left foot; 2) your left arm breaks down, so that the club drops below the parallel position (see figures 17 and 18). When either of these flaws happens, you have lost control of your club. It is swinging you instead of you swinging it.

Note that this "point of no return" (which occurs when your body cannot turn any farther), does not actually end the backswing. Your motion to this point will allow for 10 to 20 percent more backswing due to continued muscle stretching. So although your "point of no return" may seem short, your swing will actually be a little longer. Stopping while you are still in control of the club helps you maintain your tempo and your timing. When it comes time to change directions for the downswing, your move will be quicker, more powerful and under control.

Remember, your key thought with regard to swinging the club up to the top is, "I must swing the club, it must not swing me."

Many players lose the club at the top in an effort to get it farther back than they can while maintaining that essential square left wrist. Granted, it takes a lot of flexibility and suppleness to get the club back to parallel based on a full turn of the body. Remember, for some of us it just cannot be done. If you cannot do it and you insist on "cheating" on your backswing, the "rebound effect" from your left arm and wrist collapsing will cause all the coiling you have worked for to break down. Then you almost have to swing out and across the ball, slapping at it mainly with your hands and arms.

One final note on this point: most amateurs worry that if they coordinate their arms to stop swinging when their hips and shoulders stop moving back, their total backswing will be shorter and they will not be able to hit the ball as long as they did before. I guarantee you that if you keep in control at the top, you will hit the ball every bit as long or longer than before, and you will not lose all that energy to the rebound effect.

Thus, in order to retain your coil, your square left wrist and your timing, your backswing should stop when you can no longer turn your shoulders and your hips. Notice I said hips! I believe that the hips do not automatically turn with the shoulders. I have seen many golfers who make a reasonably good shoulder-turn while their hips were just sliding laterally. Failing to turn your hips can cause a reverse tilt of the upper body, with your weight moving onto the left side at the top. Therefore, I repeat that for your hips to turn, you must *make* them turn. *A good backswing turn calls for conscious turning of both your shoulders and your hips.* (See figure 19.)

Figure 17

Figure 18

Figure 19

Let's stop and take inventory at this point. After setting up with a solid grip, stance, posture and alignment, you have taken the club away with a motion initiated by the hips and shoulders so that you have pushed the clubhead "into the mitt." From there, you have continued to turn your body along a relatively upright plane, so that the club moves up in an arc around your neck rather than around your chest or shoulders. When you have turned your body as far as you can while rolling your weight onto the inside of your right foot, you resist the urge to swing your arms back "just a little more." Through it all, you have retained a flat left wrist so that the club has not flipped or wavered at any point in the swing.

There. You have completed all the elements of an excellent backswing. Next, with just one tiny move, you will unleash this fully coiled position into the start of the downswing, which is the subject of the next chapter.

9 The Key to the Downswing

Start down with a ''bump''

All of our discussion to this point has led us to the ''reaction'' portion of the swing—the downswing. I really believe that the better you execute your setup fundamentals, your takeaway and your move to the top of the swing, the more automatic your downswing will become. You will not have to worry about manipulating your hands, arms or the clubface in order to return it to square at impact. You have coiled your body to get the club to the top of the backswing, avoiding the ''cheating'' backswing that I described in the previous chapter. So there is no need to give in to the *hit impulse* and to try to create more power with your upper body. You have already stored plenty on the backswing. All you really need to do is make one small move to start the downswing, a move that will unleash the energy that you have stored so far.

You should begin your downswing with a lateral movement of your lower body toward the target. What, precisely, does this move entail? I have had most success teaching players how to start the downswing by telling them to mentally connect the movement of their left knee with their left hip and move them as follows.

Push your hip, thigh and knee laterally to the left, making a ''lateral-left bump'' along a line parallel to the target line. Your left foot should roll back, so that even if you raised it at all during the backswing, it is now flat on the ground. This first move of the downswing bears a remarkable resemblance to the dance of about ten years ago called ''the bump.''

Now, I don't know how old you are or what kind of music or dancing you like, so it is quite possible that you are not familiar with this move. During this dance, partners would stand facing in the same direction and slide their weight laterally toward each other, making contact at the hip and thigh in rhythm with the music. Now, that ''bump'' is exactly the move I want you to start your downswing with! Just imagine that you are the partner on the right, so that you are shifting your weight and ''bumping'' to the left as you start your downswing.

A common misconception among golfers regarding this move to start the downswing is the belief that you should spin your lower body, immediately turning the left hip back and to the rear, rather than bumping it laterally toward the target. Although you may time this spinning move correctly, the problem is that is also induces your upper body to spin too fast, so that your shoulders pull the clubhead outside the line of flight.

The bump allows you to transfer your weight onto your left side and hold your upper right side behind the ball as you head toward impact—the movements that are behind the expressions "late hit" and "power zone". The left side holds back the right, allowing the power to build up and explode through impact, with the follow-through shifting the weight almost completely onto the left side. (For the correct bumping action to start the downswing, see figure 20.)

When you allow your left side to turn immediately to the left to start the downswing, this movement also forces your shoulders to turn to the left too soon, and the upper body, instead of being held back, moves out and over and across the ball, a fault commonly referred to as "spinning out."

When you spin out, it is easy to hit the ball off-line in either direction. If, when your shoulders move out and over the ball, you sense that you will pull the shot, you might "hold" your release—that is, keep it from happening altogether. Timing a "holding" action is very difficult. The usual result will be a late hit with the ball sailing to the right (and with a loss of distance as well). If on the other hand you release the club normally as you spin out, the ball will inevitably start to the left of the target and go farther left during its flight.

This flaw is another good example of how the same move, in this case a spin-out of the hips rather than a bump, does not always lead to the same results. The flaw that encourages one player to slice, may make another pull or hook. So let me remind you that when you have problems and are unsure how to solve them, see your professional and let him help you find the answer. What stopped your best friend from slicing may not stop you from doing so. In fact, because you both may be slicing for different reasons, his adjustment may make your slice worse. Remember that there are no patented answers to curing a problem. Each case is unique and, as such, can have a different solution.

That digression complete, let me add a few more thoughts on the proper downswing move. The lateral left bump, coupled with a steady head and upper body, keeps your head slightly back behind the ball and causes your upper body to tilt just slightly to the right. This action will cause your arms to drop down behind you, setting them in a position from where they will return the clubhead to the ball from inside to along the target line. I liken this dropping action of the hands and arms at the start of the downswing to the movement you make in pulling the chain of an overhead light.

Once your bump initiates your weight shift, your upper body tilt and the dropping of your arms, your hips can then begin turning. Indeed, your left hip does begin to move behind you, but only after the bump. Then the weight transfer

Figure 20

from the right side to the left pulls your arms, hands and the club to the ball at impact.

As you start down, you should have no thought whatsoever of applying any force to the shot with your right side, hand or arm. They will do so without your having to worry about it. Think only of bumping your weight to the left. This move, on top of the tight coil you built at the top of the backswing, will create so much centrifugal force that you probably could not stop your right side from releasing through impact if you tried. You will not have to ask yourself "when" it is the right time to hit through the shot with your right hand and side. It will become a "happening" rather than something you try to consciously control. Let's face it, with the clubhead moving at close to or over 100 miles per hour as it contacts the ball, trying to direct the clubface at the target by manipulating it with your hands is an impossibility.

Countless students have asked me, "When do I release my hands on the shot?" My answer is to start down with the bump after making a strong back-swing coil, and the rest of the downswing becomes automatic. Just let it go.

This is the beauty of putting in all the effort on the fundamentals. You have turned your body into a tightly coiled spring, with the aim of releasing the club at your predetermined target. The bump provides a split-second of added tension that is actually a bit more than your physique can withstand. So, it releases the tension automatically, and your clubhead whips through the ball with increasing speed.

If you need to concentrate on any one thing once you have made the bump, I would suggest that you make sure you keep your head and shoulders in place, resisting any urge to "use" them to add power to the shot. Believe me, moving your head and shoulders in the direction of the target will serve only to reduce your power, not add to it, because it will interfere with the buildup of centrifugal force. In addition, if you fail to keep your swing center (the nape of your neck) steady, you are much less likely to hit the shot squarely. And a square hit is the most important factor of all in obtaining maximum distance and accuracy.

The downswing is, in my opinion, the simplest part of the golf swing. Start practicing that lateral bump toward the target with your weight moving solidly onto your left foot, while keeping your body in place behind the ball. Then, *let* yourself rather than *make* yourself unwind into the ball for solid impact. Then you are ready to follow through in fine style.

10 Impact and Follow-through

Finish erect and play well longer

You are letting it go through impact. Your hands are flying up to and then beyond their original address position as your clubhead moves from inside, to squarely on the target line for solid impact with the ball, to inside the target line again. What movements will bring you through impact and up to a balanced, relaxed follow-through position?

Once your left hip and knee have bumped and your left side holds your upper body back, your right side can move in a down-and-under motion through impact. When your right shoulder works down and under your chin, your shoulders tilt slightly to the right; consequently, your head also drops slightly to the right. At this point (which is actually prior to impact), your body is moving into what I call the "Reverse C" position (see figure 21).

You can determine this position by standing with your back to the sun or a floodlight and watching your shadow as you swing through impact. If your timing and bump are correct, you will see that as your hip moves to the left, your head falls a little to the right. Your shoulders tilt more, with the left going higher, and you will see the left side of your body bowing so that the shadow forms a reverse of the letter "C."

Let me interject a caution at this point. The Reverse C at impact is desirable in that it creates leverage and power, but it is not something you should force. This position should be a natural result of the bump to the left and right side holding back and working under. Forcing an exaggerated Reverse C carries with it two pitfalls.

First, if you force the right side back and down too much, you will also be forcing your hands (and the club) to move too far inside the target line. Thus, when your hips finally begin to turn and pull your hands through impact, they come close to colliding. One of two things happens from there: a) if you maintain the late hit you hit a blocked shot to the right; or b) if your mind senses that the "block" is coming and you hurry your release, you then become susceptible to the pull or duck hook, which can occur if the upper body stays back too far or too long. I discuss this fault in detail in the next chapter.

Second, a big Reverse C will become more and more difficult to execute as you get older. Age brings on stiffness, reducing flexibility and suppleness. It will take a progressively more strenuous effort to make this bowing move. That is when the old back starts hurting.

For this reason, when I see golfers on the lesson tee swinging with a big Reverse C, I ask them to try to cut it down—even if they are youngsters. As you get older and begin to have trouble moving into the Reverse C position, you will be forced to make some swing changes. So, to avoid the necessity of changing after perhaps fifteen or twenty years of playing, you should not use an overly-exaggerated Reverse C from the start. After all, fundamentalism requires that your spine be erect at address, at the top of the backswing and then on into the finish.

To back up my point, just look at the impact positions of players who have enjoyed longevity. Look at Sam Snead, Gene Littler, Byron Nelson, Art Wall and Tom Weiskopf. They all have Reverse C's as they near the impact position; however, none is exaggerated at the finish.

So at impact, your left side is bowed into a mild Reverse C position, holding the upper torso back behind the ball. Now, your object should be to finish in a well-balanced "T" position—shoulders vertical and body erect or perpendicular to the ground, like the letter "T." Once you are about midway into your follow-through, your upper torso should start moving toward that erect position you want to finish with. About 90 percent of your weight should be on the outside of your left foot, while your right foot has rotated to the left with only your toe remaining on the ground. Although almost all your weight is on your left, you still need that right toe there to maintain good balance.

I might add that, concerning the right foot finish, I have seen many players slide their right foot along the ground, toward their left foot as they drive onto their left side and through the ball. The most prominent current PGA Tour player who uses this move is Greg Norman, and he is certainly a tremendous golfer. However, I do not recommend the move for the simple reason that if your right foot is sliding, your entire body has to be susceptible to either moving a little too soon, which disrupts your timing, or moving past the ball. Both have a negative effect on the direction and power of the shot. Your timing has to be perfect, and for a weekend golfer, that is highly unlikely.

When a player slides his right foot toward the target, he usually does so because his stance is too wide to begin with; the move becomes necessary so that he can get his weight over and onto his left side. However, I believe that to be in the best position at impact and in the best balance at the finish, your right foot should rotate so that the toe is pointing down into the ground—the entire foot should not slide laterally.

Figure 21

Here is a good checkpoint. At the top of your well-balanced T finish, you should be able to return to your address position, allowing your right foot to roll back into the exact same spot that it occupied at address.

How should your arms, hands and club move into the finish?

The supination of your hands described in chapter 8 continues to and through impact to the point where your right hand is moving on top of your left as your arms extend to about waist-high, parallel to the ground. Once your arms and the club are outstretched, parallel to the ground, they will begin to fold at the elbow as the club swings up and over your left shoulder. At this point in the finish, the momentum generated by the clubhead being pulled back and over the shoulder causes your body to again move into somewhat of a Reverse C position. Again, as at impact, you should strive to remain as erect as possible.

Looking at players who have maintained repetitive, highly efficient swings for a long period of time, I have noticed that along with a full yet *erect* finish position, they also finish with the shaft of their own club either parallel to the ground or very close to parallel (see figure 22). They finish in a position that looks like a letter "T"; that is, the body, which is erect, forms the base of the letter, and the clubshaft, which is parallel to the ground, behind the head, "crosses" the T.

I am convinced that this parallel finish of the club is a key to these players' longevity. Let me explain why. A few years ago I used to finish my own swing with the shaft pointing much more downward than parallel to the ground. At that point, pain shot through my right hip with every full swing. I decided to work toward finishing with the club closer to parallel to the ground, which would mean that my hips were turning in a more circular fashion after impact. A good model of this type of parallel finish is the finish of the PGA Tour's Danny Edwards or Greg Norman.

This change immediately reduced the amount of strain and tension on my lower back. With this finish, I can practice as much as I want and play every day with no strain or pain. I know that this finish is adding to my own longevity as a golfer and I am sure it will do the same for you.

If you have experienced lower back problems during your swing, check the position of your clubshaft at the finish. If you are not finishing with the club parallel to the ground, work on it, and you will feel the difference.

The last point I want to make about your finish position is that when your arms and hands bring the club to the finish, they must remain firmly in command. Remember the key saying we mentioned regarding the backswing: "I must swing the club, the club does not swing me." This saying applies to the finish position just as it does to the top of the backswing. If you let your arms swing to a finish that is loose and limp, the club will be out of control—and most likely it will bounce off your left shoulder. The club's weight and momentum could then pull you off-balance and you could fall backwards. This is a problem

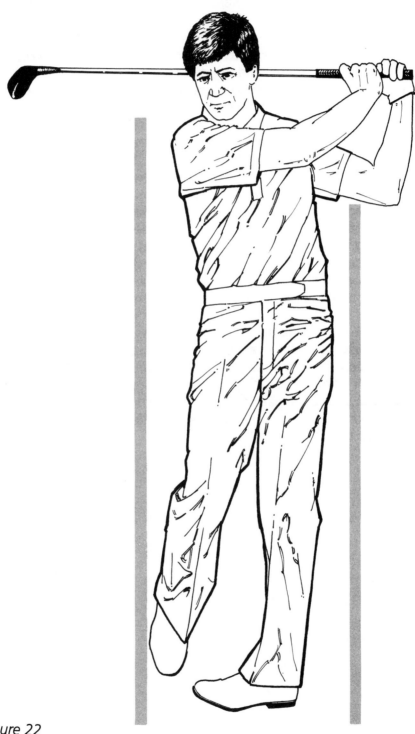

Figure 22

for some golfers; in fact, I have even seen a shaft snap as a result of bouncing off a player's shoulder.

So finish your swing in an erect position, with your club parallel to the ground, your body in good balance and your hands in complete control of the club. You must be in control of yourself and the club at all times.

I repeat: the fundamental approach details the ultimate fundamentals and moves of the golf swing, but it does not expect you to be able to perform each and every motion to the letter. Instead, I ask you to study and understand the moves, and work to make your golf swing incorporate them as closely as you are mentally and physically capable of doing.

Remember, you are you and I am me. We are different in size, shape, intellect, coordination and ability. The laws of physics are unchangeable. The fundamentals are designed to place your body in the ideal position to contact the ball with speed and precision. For you, the ideal position is the one you can best get into and best swing from.

So, be a fundamentalist and work at having a good grip, stance, posture and alignment. You will see that the swing moves discussed in this chapter will become easier to perform, and your shots will improve along with your score.

Now that you have a fundamentally sound swing, you are *almost* ready to move into the parts of golf that are *really* fun: the shotmaking and strategy that will transform you from a good swinger to an all-around *player*. Before we move into these areas, though, let's take some time to discuss the most common pitfalls and misconceptions regarding the golf swing. Doing so will provide valuable insurance that will enable you to solve minor problems if and when they crop up in your swing.

11 Swing Fault Misconceptions

"I picked my head up"

Throughout years of teaching and playing, it has been my experience that one of the biggest stumbling blocks keeping amateurs from improving is their failure to understand why their shots fly off-line. They lay the blame for bad shots on erroneous concepts that have become embedded in the everyday jargon of golf. I call these terms misconceptions or scapegoats. They are harmful not only because they keep the golfer from making his needed correction, but also because they can lead him farther from the path of correct fundamentals by inducing him to work on a *wrong* move. To my mind, there are eleven such misconceptions.

Misconception #1: I picked my head up. This is the most common excuse for just about every bad shot in the book. I have heard it for a variety of shots, from the "top" to the "fat" to the "skull" or "slice." It seems that whatever the bad shot is, the odds-on favorite fault cited is the picked-up head.

Well, I am going to come right out and say it: there is *no such thing* as picking up your head. I have told this to countless pupils in the past and I am telling you now.

The movement I am referring to is the one in which a player swings at the ball and jerks his head at impact in an attempt to see where the ball goes. Consider this: the physics of swinging a golf club involve centrifugal force, which is defined as a force "moving or tending to move away from the center." When you swing, all your movement is away from your swing center and toward the ball. Picking up your head would mean yanking it away from the point where all your muscles are being directed. I do not believe this action is possible as it could, literally, cause you a severe pain in the neck.

It is possible for your head to lift, but not in the way just described. What really happens is that, for a number of reasons, *your entire body* is pulled up or jerked away right at impact.

The most common reason for what is considered picked-up head is actually the tendency to use the wrong muscles to begin with. The golfer may have used his "front" muscles—forearm, bicep and chest muscles—to execute the back-swing instead of bending more and using his back muscles. Or, even if he did use his back muscles on the backswing, he may have given in to the "hit impluse" and started down with a switch to his front muscles, causing a down-swing that is a kind of throw by the arms and a lifting of the upper body.

This fault can also be due to having a too-powerful right side setup (as dis-cussed in chapter 3), standing too close to the ball, using a reverse weight-shift on the downswing and lifting onto the toes at impact. Each one of these faults results in the entire upper body being pulled up. The head itself has not lifted; it simply rises along with the body.

Misconception #2: A stiff left arm is a must. Many golfers believe they should have a stiff left arm, locked at the elbow. They think it should be as rigid as a four-by-four. If you observe the top players on the PGA Tour, you will see very few who lock their left arm at the elbow. In fact, a fair number, including Curtis Strange, play tremendous golf with a noticeably bent left arm.

You should strive for a left arm that is firm, with your muscles ready to per-form the task of holding and swinging the club with control. You need a fair degree of pressure in the last three fingers of your left hand so that the lower or "under" arm muscles are fairly tight. This way, you keep the muscles taut, yet still allow them to remain flexible. So, maintain a firm left arm, but not a stiff one (see figure 23).

Misconception #3: Be comfortable at address. This is another one of golf's most misinterpreted pieces of advice. I am going to shoot straight from the hip: there should be no such thing as being perfectly comfortable when hitting a golf ball. I maintain that if you are totally comfortable, it is highly unlikely that you can be in good posture over the ball at address.

The conscious effort of muscle-priming and proper positioning of the body in correct posture is work; therefore, the correct posture cannot be a completely relaxed or comfortable position. Because we must work at it, and it is not totally easy or natural, I think of posture as a position we must get *accustomed* to.

Now, if you say that once you get accustomed to your address position it feels more comfortable, I can accept the term "comfortable" in this context. How-ever, most people think that "comfortable" refers to a stance grip, posture or other setup element that comes easy, is relaxing and does not require a great deal of mental or physical exertion. You are just not going to feel like you are in an easy chair when you strive to be fundamentally sound. So you must work toward a better grip, stance and posture and strive to become more accustomed to them, even if they feel uncomfortable at first.

Misconception #4: Stay relaxed. Being relaxed is the sidekick of the admoni-tion to be comfortable. Most players do become tight and tense, so relaxing to some degree is needed. But the majority of amateurs overdo the extent to which they relax.

Figure 23

Watch the pros in action for big stakes on the PGA Tour. Their mannerisms are aimed at keeping themselves mentally and physically relaxed. They breathe deeply before a crucial shot. They perform practice swings, sometimes just swinging their arms without a club. The point is that yes, you must be composed and fairly relaxed, because anxiety breeds tension and tension breeds speed. The key is to relax your muscles so they will perform—not so that you will be rendered incapable of adhering to your setup and swing fundamentals. You can easily lose control over the fine precision of muscle movement that makes a golf swing.

So be relaxed, but don't lapse into the limpness and looseness that make you lose control of your body and the club.

Misconception #5: Keep your weight on your heels throughout the swing. This admonition is a carryover from a past era in golf—the 1920s and 1930s. Back then, this advice was sound. But today this adage is incorrect because of the vast differences in modern golf equipment. These scientific advances have necessitated a change in the way golfers must swing.

When golfers played with hickory-shafted clubs, they naturally had to develop fundamentals and swings that would perform optimally with that equipment. Their clubshafts were extremely whippy, with a great deal of torque—the force that produces or tends to produce a twisting motion. This rotating motion caused the clubhead to open or close at impact. Thus, players had to develop swings that accentuated one movement or the other.

In almost all instances a flat swing plane produced the best results with hickory shafts. Players swung the club on a plane that was more horizontal that vertical. Still, this equipment and the swings that went with them made consistent play difficult, even by the very best players. The problems led manufacturers on a search for something better.

The major innovation of the steel shaft did more than anything to change the fundamentals of golf. It is the key contributing factor in the development of the modern golf swing, which features a more upright swing plane. One of the first to implement this change was Byron Nelson, whom many hail as the "Father of the Modern Swing."

This more upright swing became necessary because steel shafts, much stiffer than hickory shafts, significantly reduced the amount of torque created during the swing. A flat swing could no longer return the clubhead to the ball squarely. The only way this could be done consistently was to swing in a more upright fashion, with the clubhead moving more closely to the target line throughout the swing.

With this major difference, a player's balance had to adjust. Players had to move their weight from the heels, where the weight used to be needed, to the balls of the feet, so that they could bend over at the waist more. This bending at the waist then produced a swing in which the upper body turned and coiled against the lower body on the backswing. The shoulders turned more vertically than before, and the arc of the club became more upright.

So the expression "Keep your weight on your heels" is a misrepresentation of modern fundamentals. You may still hear it advocated by older players and professionals who have not adjusted from what they originally learned. Many older golf instruction books also expound the old method of keeping the weight on the heels, so this now-incorrect axiom lives on. I hope it will no longer get in the way for you.

Misconception #6: Pause at the top of of the backswing. This principle is another holdover from the days of the evolution in equipment and the golf swing. Its basis is an optical illusion that occurred when a player changed directions at the top of the swing while using a whippy hickory shaft.

At that time, the only thing golfers had to rely on to see, analyze and teach the golf swing, is what the human eye saw. And to the naked eye, good players of that era seemed to pause at the top of their backswings. Since all good players had this apparent pause, it bacame an accepted principle of good golf to swing up to the top of the backswing, pause, then start down. Thus, golfers learned to execute the golf swing in two pieces rather than in one continuous motion. Even today, many golfers are told to make a conscious pause at the top of the swing.

However, with advances in photographic equipment, the swings of many great players were put on film, and astute teaching pros made a startling discovery. The golf swing was one continuous motion from start to finish.

I liken the golf swing to the action of a fisherman when casting with a long, flexing fly-rod. When the fisherman whips the rod back, there is a tremendous amount of flexing in the rod. This flex *increases* when he makes his first move to cast the rod back toward his target because, for an instant, the tip end of the rod is still going back while he begins to swing the grip end forward.

So, the flexing of the rod and the golf club presents an optical illusion of a pause, when in fact there is none. Do not confuse yourself by thinking that you need to pause at the top.

Misconception #7: Snap the wrists at impact, or, *When do you break the wrists?* The question I am most often asked is, "When do I break my wrists in the swing?" As an amateur, when I was less certain in my knowledge of the golf swing, I answered by saying that the wrists break, but that they break without any conscious effort. Today, after years of studying the golf swing and teaching, I have a different answer: "Good wrist action is no wrist action" (see previous chapter).

This statement really takes a lot of golfers aback. Breaking your wrists on the backswing and snapping your wrists at impact are two of the biggest false impressions of golf swing mechanics in golfers' minds today.

You might insist that if the wrists do not snap or break, they must certainly do *something.* Yes—they pronate and supinate. That is, midway through the backswing, the back of the left hand points in the same direction that you are facing. On the downswing, that same hand supinates, meaning it rolls back so that it is square to the target at impact, as it was at address. Into the finish, the left palm is vertical to the ground and in line with your left arm.

While pronation and supination do occur, remember that this movement of the wrists is *not* independent; it is a complete, one-piece rotation of the hands, wrists and arms. The wrists themselves make no independent movements, although centrifugal force does cause them to cock at the top of the backswing and uncock as the club returns to the ball. So, for all intents and purposes, good wrist action is no wrist action.

Misconception #8: The right elbow must not fly. It is true, particularly in the modern golf swing, that a flaw known as the flying right elbow certainly exists. Miller Barber's right elbow at the top of the backswing is the best example. So why is a flying right elbow listed here as a misconception?

I have listed it as such because it is a fault that has been badly misunderstood and can lead to other swing problems. Many golfers believe that the right elbow is flying whenever it does not remain tucked against the right hip or waist throughout the backswing. But if the right elbow were tucked in to this degree, the right arm would become the leader of the swing. As I have stated throughout this book, the left arm is the leader, the power arm, and the right arm is the one that should follow and go where it is forced to go. For the left arm to lead the swing while remaining firm and extended, the right cannot possibly remain tucked against the right hip. If it did, then your left arm would have to collapse at the elbow—in fact, break down completely.

For the left arm to remain completely extended, the right elbow must move away from the hip to some degree. Doesn't that mean that it is flying? No, it is not flying as long as the elbow still points toward the ground when it moves away from the hip. Your right elbow is flying if it points at or above the horizon at the top of the backswing (see figures 24 and 25).

As long as your right elbow moves away from your right side, but points toward the ground, that segment of your swing is in good shape. Let the left arm lead and remain comfortably extended, pushing your right arm away.

Misconception #9: Start the downswing by pulling the left arm. This swing thought is a carryover from the two-piece swing discussed earlier. This theory advises you to swing to the top of the backswing and, after pausing, bring the club down by pulling with the left arm.

The most efficient swing is a one-piece swing in which the arms and shoulders swing the club up to the top of the backswing. But while the club and arms are still not quite finished going back, the lower body reaches its full backswing turn. Then it automatically rebounds and moves forward toward the target, the lateral left bump in turn pulling the arms and club down—the action-reaction principle already discussed.

Figure 24

Figure 25

So, our guiding principle is that the lower body starts the arms and club down from the top. The left arm itself does not initiate the downswing—rather, it is pulled down by the lower left side. So, abandon this false prescription for starting the downswing.

Misconception # 10: "Coming over" the ball causes a hook. A misleading explanation for hitting a bad pull or hook is that the golfer "came over" the ball—that is, the head, shoulders and upper body moved ahead of the ball prior to impact.

It has been my experience over the years that almost every time this action occurs, the player hits a push or a slice, not a hook. When the head and upper body move ahead of the ball prematurely, the arms and club lag too far behind. They cannot square up to the target line at impact, so they contact the ball while still open to the target line. Result: a push or a slice.

In reality, the pull, hook or dreaded "duck hook" occur when the golfer makes the exact opposite move—that is, when he stays behind the ball too long in the downswing. If his head and upper body lay back too long, then the left arm and the clubface get to the ball too soon in relation to the rest of the body; the arm and clubhead release early, causing the clubface to be closed or aimed left of the target at impact, causing the pull or the hook.

The problem here is that the timing of the swing is off. But, contrary to the expression, coming over the ball does not cause a hook. Rather, *coming off* the ball and staying behind it with the upper body cause the problem.

Misconception # 11: "What helped you will help me." This statement does not refer to a specific swing fault, but to an error in thinking about swing corrections that amateurs make all the time. Let's say that Player A just got a lesson from his professional to correct a problem with hooking. Player B, a friend, also has the same problem, so A immediately gives B his lesson. Both players think that since it cured A it has to be the answer for B.

I can assure you that different players hook (or slice) for different reasons. There are as many swings as there are golfers, and there are no pat answers for problems. What helped A may not, in fact probably will not, help B. A might have a bad grip at the root of his hook, while B may have bad posture, poor alignment or any number of other variables that cause *his* hook.

The same effect does not always emanate from the same cause. In fact, I would go so far as to say that sometimes the same cause, for example a "hook" grip, can cause opposite effects. One player hooks with this grip, yet another, because of his particular set of compensations, slices the ball.

Though your professional has solved your problem, this answer is not for everyone whose shots have the same end result as yours. The only thing that is right for everyone is to get as close as possible to executing the four fundamentals and to work with the swing that comes from a good setup.

Part 3
Shotmaking and Strategy

12 Keys to Straight and Long Wood Play

A good driver never breaks a tee

Let's begin our examination of the facets of shotmaking by looking at play with the longest club in the bag—the driver. Ben Hogan has stated that the driver is the most critical club in the bag because it really determines the way you play the rest of the hole. On most par fours, a well-hit drive into the fairway sets you up to shoot to the green with a middle or perhaps a short iron, and thus have a reasonable shot at a par or birdie. A good drive on a par five may even give you a chance to go for the green in two.

However, if you drive into trouble—woods, rough or fairway bunker—a par will be hard-earned and a bogey the more likely result. Should your drive end up in a water hazard or out of bounds, then you will be struggling for either a bogey or double bogey. So in an off-beat kind of way, I think that the expression "drive for show" is actually true—if you want to "show" a par or birdie on your card, you had better hit your drive in the fairway!

Let's discuss the setup for your normal tee shot, one for which you do not need to hit the ball particularly high or low, or curve the shot in either direction.

Most golfers do not tee the ball up high enough. Tee the ball up with a minimum of one-half resting above the top of a soled driver. With the ball elevated to this degree, you can hit it just a bit on the upswing—exactly what you want. Remember that the loft on the average driver is only 10 or 11 degrees. It is very tough to get a good trajectory on a tee shot if you hit *down* on it with such a small amount of loft. You want to sweep the ball with the driver when it is just past the bottom of your swing arc—definitely not on the downswing!

A proper hit should leave the tee in the ground or, if the club hits the tee, pulled out of the ground. A good driver *never* breaks his tees in half, an indication that he is sawing them off with a downward-moving arc like the one that should only be used with a short iron. If anything, the good driver will chip away the top of the tee until it can no longer hold a ball—but he will never break one in half.

Now that you have teed the ball properly, establish your aiming line to the target. Then line up the club perpendicular to the target line, with your body square or parallel to your target line (review chapter 3 on alignment, if necessary).

With the driver, you should place the ball more forward in your stance than for any other club—between your left heel and instep. This positioning helps you strike the ball while the club is moving on its upward path.

Regarding your stance for the driver, I suggest you place your right foot directly under your right shoulder. Place your left foot slightly outside of or to the left of your left shoulder. The belief that the inside of both feet should be as far apart as the width of the outside of the shoulders is not quite accurate. Instead, I teach that you should place your right foot directly under your right shoulder, rather than outside it. When your right foot is directly underneath your right shoulder, your weight shifts directly over and onto the right leg, and your knee is also directly over your right foot at the top of the backswing.

When your entire right leg points straight up instead of "slanting up," as it would if your right foot were placed outside your shoulder, there are a number of benefits. First, the position reduces sway. If your foot is outside your shoulder line, you tend to sway in order to get your weight onto your right side. Also, the philosophy of swinging back against a firm right leg and thigh actually induces a push to the left, resulting in an *end-of-the backswing reverse tilt,* which occurs when the tension becomes so great in your right thigh that it pushes your upper body weight back to the left at the top of the backswing—a reverse tilt.

Now, when your weight shifts onto your right leg and foot, which are directly under your right shoulder, you guarantee yourself a solid brace and foundation for support at the top of the backswing, as well as a strong springboard to drive off to the left as you start the downswing.

Your stance with the driver should be square or parallel to your target line, or just a touch closed. With the ball more forward in your stance, the clubface is slightly into the upswing at impact—and points slightly to the left of the line drawn across your toes as it contacts the ball. Standing a touch closed allows you to hit the ball on the upswing and still hit it on target.

Now let's go over your weight distribution and posture for the address with the driver. Your weight should be neutral or evenly distributed between your feet, with your upper body tilted slightly to the right. You should be leaning in the direction of the swing motion, that is, toward the ball, so your weight must be forward, toward the balls of your feet. Taller players, due to their height, will place their weight a little more toward the ankles than will shorter players, due to the erectness of their posture. But all golfers should always feel light on their heels.

Your spine should be erect, yet bent over the ball. Your hips should protrude outward, your knees should be flexed and your arms dropped and extended.

Your muscle tone should be fairly firm and taut, rather than loose and sloppy, so that you are primed and ready to swing.

What about the adjustments you need to make when you face special shot-making situations off the tee? The first is the high tee shot that you want to hit when the hole is playing downwind. Your first move is to tee the ball higher than normal—say, a quarter of an inch higher. This adjustment allows you to contact the ball with more of the mass of the clubhead *beneath* the ball's equator, helping you launch it into a much steeper starting trajectory. The end result is that you get the maximum benefit from that tailwind.

When driving downwind, lean your lower body a little more to the left and your upper body a little bit more to the right. This shift helps you make a more shallow-bottomed swing and allows you to sweep the ball off the tee on the upswing more than normal.

When driving downwind you may want to hit a fade or cut shot, which leaves the clubface slightly open at impact. An open face adds loft to the club and height to the shot. Be sure to aim a little left of your target to compensate for the ball drifting to the right. Just a little, though—the tailwind will tend to straighten out any sidespin on the ball, so it will not curve that much.

One final point on the downwind tee shot: do not try to kill it! Everything is in your favor. All you want to do is make a smooth, easy swing and launch the shot at a higher-than-normal angle. If you normally hit the ball low, you might even hit the downwind tee shot farther by using a 3-wood to help get the ball up quickly.

Next is the low drive into the wind. Your teeing procedures here should be just the opposite of those for the downwind shot. Some instructors teach that you should tee the ball at the same height whether you hit upwind or downwind, but I do not agree. I believe you should tee the ball lower when going into the wind—so that only a quarter of the ball rests above the soled clubface. This way, more of the mass of the clubhead will be *above* the ball's equator, making the ball start out on a much lower trajectory so that you "cheat" the wind of as much of its effect on the ball as possible.

Move the ball back slightly in your stance, to just inside your left heel. This position will allow you to contact the ball just before or at the bottom of your swing, again helping to start the shot off low. Lean your entire body a little left at address, with about 10 percent more weight on your left side than normal.

When you are ready to take the club back, stay relaxed and swing easily. Do not fight the wind, tense up or overpower the ball, or you will hit a pop-up or even a topped shot. You must remain steady over the ball throughout the swing. Another benefit of swinging easily is that you put a minimum amount of backspin on the ball, so that it will not rise as much later in its flight. These "upshooters," caused by excessive backspin, are the shots that really get devoured by a headwind. So play it smart, swing easily and put less backspin on the ball. It will bore through the wind like a bullet.

You can also set up for a draw or a hook when teeing off into the wind. This shot calls for a closed clubface at address and at impact, which delofts the club and helps keep the ball down. Drawn or hooked shots also run farther when they hit the ground. Be sure to aim your body as much to the right as you plan for the ball to curve left. Also remember that a headwind will increase the effect of any sidespin on the ball. If you plan to make the shot curve, figure on it curving more than it would normally.

What about driving in crosswinds? First, you must decide on your approach because you can do one of two things. The first and probably the simpler approach is to "use" the wind by aiming far enough to the side it is blowing from that it will carry your ball back to the middle of the fairway. The second approach is to hit "into" the crosswind; that is, aim down the center of the fairway, drawing the ball into a crosswind from the left or fading it into a crosswind from the right. The result is that the ball "fights" the crosswind and holds its line.

Which of these methods should you choose? If you want to obtain maximum distance on the shot and no trees impede your starting line of flight so that you have the room to start your ball right or left to adjust for the curve, then "use" the wind. Be sure to adjust your aiming line as much to the right or left as you feel the wind will curve your ball. Then use your normal setup and swing. This is the simplest way to play the shot—you aim to hit a straight shot and let the wind add the curve. The ball will fly and roll a little farther than it would if there were no wind. The strategy of "working" the ball so it holds its line against the wind is good in certain circumstances. For example, you may need to make the ball settle down quickly, as when you hit to a narrow or sloping fairway that is well-bunkered or guarded by a water hazard. This is a very controlled tee shot for which you must stay very steady and not try to overpower the ball. Aim your body down the center but adjust your clubface, left for a draw or right for a fade, the amount needed to counteract the strength of the wind from left or right. It also helps to keep the ball low, so play it back in your stance an inch as well. Then swing normally.

Let's move on now to the fairway woods. How much difference is there between hitting a wood shot from the fairway or light rough and hitting a drive from the tee? I believe that your stance, posture, hand position and weight distribution for fairway woods should be exactly the same as they are for the driver. The only change you should make is in ball position. Adjust your stance so that the ball is slightly farther to the right, positioned opposite your left heel.

Because the ball is resting on the ground rather than on a tee, you should make contact with it slightly sooner, at the very bottom of your swing arc or just before that point. (Keep in mind that this lowest point in the swing does vary a bit from player to player, depending on the strength of your lateral downswing shift.)

Fairway wood shots should be contacted right at the base of the swing because of the minimal amount of loft on these clubs. Yes, the fairway woods have more loft than the driver, but the club must contact the ball while it is resting on the ground. By positioning the ball farther back, off the left heel, you ensure that you get "all" of the ball, yet have no trouble getting the ball nicely airborne.

You will encounter "problem lies" at times when you need to hit a fairway wood. Let's say you have a "tight" lie—the ball is lying very close to the actual surface of the ground, with little or no cushion of grass beneath it. Most amateurs are scared of this shot, afraid that they cannot get the ball up in the air. It is not that tough! Actually, with little grass around the ball, you have an excellent chance to strike the shot cleanly and with control.

First, move the ball slightly back in your stance, about two inches behind a spot opposite your left heel. This allows you to make contact while the clubhead is still slightly on the descent. Stand a touch closer to the ball than usual. You will automatically make a backswing that is a little more upright than usual, so your downswing angle of attack is steeper, allowing you to pinch or nip the ball sooner. You should feel like you're hitting down on the ball, as you do with a middle iron shot.

By hitting down you deloft the clubface a few degrees, so that the flight of the ball is lower on any shot from a tight lie. The cure is simple—just use a more lofted wood. Hit a 4-wood instead of a 3-wood, for example. You will get the same distance as you normally would with a 3-wood because of the delofted position of the clubface at impact.

Remember to maintain your left wrist angle, keeping your arms and wrists firm, with the hands leading the clubhead through impact. At impact, you should feel as though you are nipping the ground. Contact of the club with the ground will be short and shallow. You do not want the clubhead to bounce off the ground before it contacts the ball, causing a topped shot, or open or close the clubface, causing a hook or a slice.

When played out of the rough the fairway wood is a different shot entirely. First, evaluate the lie carefully to make sure you can get the ball out. Actually, you can hit lofted woods out of rough that you think is too deep or too thick. The main thing is to be sure that the launch angle of the ball from the clubface is sufficient to get the ball up and out.

For hitting from rough, you should consider carrying one more of the lofted or utility woods—the 5-, 6-, 7- or 8-woods. These clubs have thick, heavy sole plates that put the center of gravity very low on the clubface for the purpose of digging the ball out of just such lies.

Basically, your number-one priority is to be sure to use enough loft to get the

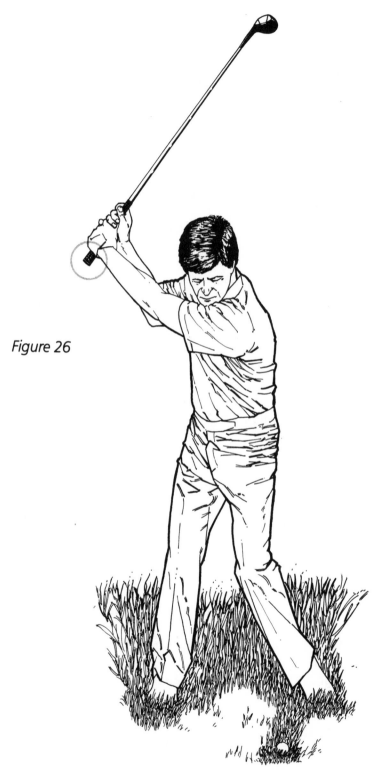

Figure 26

ball up and out. Once you have picked a club, place the ball farther back in your stance so you can hit the ball more on the downswing, thus keeping the muffling effect of the grass between club and ball to a minimum. Choke up slightly on the club and hover it slightly above the ball, so you will not get the club caught in the grass on your backswing. Pick the club up a bit more so your backswing is more upright and your downswing angle of attack is even steeper than usual. Depending on the severity of the lie, you may feel that you need to cock your wrists a bit to enable you to make a descending blow with a minimum of grass getting in the way (see figure 26).

Through impact, hold on firmly with your left hand in particular. If you do not, the grass will tend to grab the clubhead and spin it, usually closing the face so that the ball squirts left. Even with a firm hold, the face will likely close a bit at impact, so aim right of target to adjust for the pull you anticipate. Also, expect the ball to come out lower than usual and to run when it lands.

If your ball is really buried in rough, play it smart and dig it out with an iron. It is better to be safely out of rough and short of the green, than sorry after having topped or fluffed the shot 15 yards so it is still in the rough.

So, there are the keys to shotmaking with woods—now let's consider the keys to high-quality shotmaking with your irons.

13 Iron Play Expertise

Change positions but not your swing

Good iron play is nearly as important as driving the ball well off the tee. Once you have put the ball in play successfully, you need to feel confident that you will hit the greens in regulation. Assuming you have driven it a good distance down the fairway, you should have every expectation of putting your approach shot onto the green with a reasonable shot at a birdie.

Let's break the irons down into three segments or areas. The long irons are numbers 1, 2 and 3; the medium or mid-irons are numbers 4, 5 and 6; the short irons are the 7-iron through the sand wedge.

For all iron shots you should strive for certain constants. Your posture and grip should never change; neither should your tempo and timing. However, there are several changes that should take place depending on the particular shot at hand. These are in the areas of ball position, width of your stance and weight distribution.

You should adjust the ball position in your stance according to the club you are hitting. Another school of thought on ball position says that you should play the ball off your left heel for all shots and simply widen your stance as the clubs get longer. But I feel that this system is dangerous because most players are not supple enough to implement it. They do not have the lower leg drive to the left side to play the ball from this forward position with all their clubs. They find it too difficult to keep the head steady and behind the ball and still make solid contact with a descending short-iron blow. They are more susceptible to hitting a skulled or bladed shot or, alternatively, moving their upper bodies too fast so that they get ahead of the shot and push it to the right.

Let's look at why I prefer that you adjust your ball position. First, as I have said, the swing arc is basically a circle. The very bottom of the circle of the swing is just in front of the center of the stance. The short irons have sufficient loft to hit the ball with a downward blow and still get it airborne while playing the ball from the center of the stance. But as you progress through the 6-, 5- and 4-irons, the clubs have less loft, about 4 degrees less with each club. You need to move the ball slightly more forward so you do not strike it with so much of a downward blow.

Starting with the 6-iron, your ball position should move slightly left, about one inch for each successive club. In this way you still hit down slightly on the longer irons. This position combined with the loft of these clubs, is more than sufficient to get a rising flight that drops the ball relatively softly on the green.

The width of your stance is another important consideration in the successful execution of your iron shots. If stance width is correct, it solidifies your balance and effects a good weight transfer. With the right foot positioned directly under your right shoulder, a good hip- and shoulder-turn puts your weight immediately onto that right leg. You adjust the left foot to different widths to fit the club you are using.

An old and widely accepted axiom suggests keeping the distance between the insides of the feet equal to your shoulder width for a 5-iron shot. I think the proper width for a 5-iron should be just a little narrower than that—the outside edges of your feet should be equal to the width of your shoulders. Your stance should be a touch wider for each longer club, and subsequently your stance for the shorter clubs should be a shade narrower with each successive club.

As the irons get shorter, your stance, in addition to getting narrower, should open slightly. You should drop your left foot back away from your aiming line a little more as the loft increases. The reason for this opening is to allow more room for your hips to clear as your legs drive to the left side and your hands move through impact.

Let's look at some shotmaking concerns with the long, middle and short irons. For your basic shot with a long iron (1, 2 or 3), place the ball slightly back in your stance from where the ball would be with the driver, or a little inside your left heel. Your stance should be square or parallel to your line of flight, or just a touch open. The outside edges of your feet should be slightly wider than the width of your shoulders. As with the driver, your weight distribution should be neutral, that is, evenly balanced between your feet.

When you swing a long iron, your most useful swing thought will be to keep your tempo slow and smooth throughout. And I stress the word *throughout*. Most golfers find it fairly simple to take the club back slowly and smoothly, but doing so when starting down and coming through the shot is an entirely different propostion. Try to imagine that a long iron shot is nothing more than a longer 7-iron (or whatever iron club you have lots of confidence in). Then, try to swing with the same tempo as you would with that shorter iron.

I think that we should be realistic at this point and admit that, even with sound technique, some players who do not generate a lot of clubhead speed are likely to have some difficulty obtaining the needed height or distance with the long irons. If this happens to you even after you have improved your swing technique, you should consider switching to the 5-, 6- and 7-woods. They are a great alternative because they get the ball up much more easily, especially out of the rough. Ladies, juniors, seniors and high handicappers will most likely play better golf using the utility woods instead of the long irons. Don't ever feel like you have to play with clubs you don't hit well.

Now for the basic shot with the middle irons. Place the ball left-of-center in your stance, but to the right of your left heel. Your stance should be slightly more open than for the long irons, and your weight distribution should again be evenly balanced between the feet. When executing the swing, remember to keep your tempo smooth and your action compact. *Always feel as if you can swing the club back a little farther than you actually are.*

For the short irons, the 7-iron through the sand wedge, you should place the ball in the dead center of your stance, which becomes a little more open than with the medium irons. Your stance will also get narrower as the clubs increase in loft because the shorter the club, the narrower your swing arc and the narrower your base of support must be. Narrowing and opening the stance is a good insurance policy against overswinging.

Your basic swing for the various irons is in order. Notice that there is really no difference in the way you actually swing the club for a long iron or a short iron. Only the positioning of your body at address differs. That difference becomes even more evident as we move on to the real shotmaking aspects of hitting the irons—hitting the draws and fades you need to work the ball close to the pin. To draw or fade you must adjust your setup in a way that will cause your arms to swing on a flatter or more upright plane.

Let's discuss the draw first. You must increase your left arm extension so that it is slightly farther away from your body, putting it more in the "power" position. Extending your left arm automatically sets you up to swing the club on a slightly flatter plane. It also slightly closes your shoulders to the target line to promote a swing plane in which the club contacts the ball while moving from inside the target line. Assuming that you swing the club freely so that you release the clubhead fully at impact, you will end up imparting more sidespin on the ball without consciously changing your swing, only your setup. Of course, you must also compensate by lining your body up slightly to the right of the pin.

To fade your shots, put your right arm in more of an extended or "power" position and stand a little closer to the ball, so that your upper body is more erect and your takeaway and swing plane are more upright. The upright plane causes your arms and the club to lift up and just slightly outside your line of flight with little or no clockwise rotation of the hands and arms. From this position, you pull the club down slightly across the ball with your clubface square or a trifle open, so there is left-to-right sidespin on the ball. Again, you should adjust your alignment, aiming left of the pin to provide for drift on the ball to the right. Remember also that the fade will fly a little higher, softer and shorter than the draw, so you must take plenty of club and swing smoothly.

What about playing on a windy day when you want to keep your iron shots low to lessen the wind's effect? Well, the "punch" or "knockdown" shot is very valuable to have with your middle to short irons. Here's how to execute it.

First, move the ball slightly back in your stance from its usual position. Widen your stance a little for greater balance and stability. Your weight should be slightly more on your left foot than normal. Whenever you play the knockdown shot, choose at least one and probably two clubs more than you ordinarily would. Choke up on the grip. Make a three-quarter swing with little weight shift. Pull down and through firmly, with your left arm in control, and follow through low so that your club winds up pointing at the target.

Because you have played the ball back in your stance, the ball will most likely draw, so adjust your aiming line to the right as much as you feel the ball will move left. You can also hold your release on a punch shot so that it also becomes a cut shot. Here you would aim a little left of your target. Because the shot will fly a little higher, take one club longer than for the knockdown with a draw. For any punch shot, accuracy and balance are vital. You must not try to overpower the shot. Take plenty of club and swing under control.

The high, soft shot is great to have when the pin is cut just over a bunker or a water hazard, or when you are hitting downwind. You want a shot that descends as softly as possible so it can clear the hazard safely, yet not roll too far past the hole.

Whatever club you use, move the ball about two inches forward or to the left of the standard ball position for that club. Your stance should be of normal width and your weight distributed evenly between your feet, or even favoring the right a little. Select the same club as normally, or one less if you are hitting downwind.

To hit the ball high and soft, set up to hit a slight cut or fade. Adjust your aiming line a little left of parallel to the target line to allow for the ball sliding right. Keeping the clubface square to the target means it will be slightly open in relation to your stance.

Your swing thought for this shot is that the swing should feel long and even somewhat lazy. You want to feel as if you will scoop the ball off the ground. You may need to feel as if your hands, especially your right, are more active in working down, under and then up into the follow-through than on a normal iron shot. As always, tempo and balance are important, and staying behind the ball is critical.

One question about iron play that many amateurs ask is, "How much of a divot should I take?" Well, the divot varies depending on the shot. You will take more of a divot with your short irons than your long ones. In general, a "good" divot is somewhat long and shallow, even to the point of being curved. That is, it should be shallow at the start, getting deeper at its center and then shallowing out again as the club rises up in the follow-through. You should feel as if you are tearing or pulling the grass out of the ground, not digging it out.

You can learn a great deal from your divots (or lack of them) in playing your iron shots. Divots that aim left of target, for example, indicate too steep an angle of attack on the ball, usually caused by poor timing of your upper body. When your upper body moves ahead of your lower body, it causes the club to approach the ball from outside the target line. The result is almost always a slice.

Divots that point to the right of your target indicate that on the downswing you have swung the club from too far on the inside. A blocked or pushed shot usually results, although you can get a bad pull or a duck hook if your release your hands quickly at impact.

Very deep divots also indicate too steep an angle of attack. They usually result from the same causes as the left-pointing divot. They also indicate that your legs may be bending too much or your shoulders collapsing, meaning you are lunging at the ball. Alternatively, deep divots could mean that your clubs are too long, or simply that you are standing too close to the ball.

Many amateurs take no divot at all on their iron shots. This is usually the result of using your "front" muscles and lifting through impact, raising your upper body as if to scoop or help the ball up. Standing too far from the ball also causes this problem. If your clubs happen to be too short, this position will also make you hit the ball thin, without any divot.

You can really learn a lot about your swing by watching your divots. If they are consistent in depth and directed at the target, you have a good indication that your swing is consistent and well-balanced. If you know what to look for, any variation will clue you in to the malady.

You now have a greater understanding of the proper setup and swing adjustments you need to be a varied shotmaker with both your woods and irons. You now have the "weapons" with which to attack the golf course. It is time to discuss the strategy you need to produce your best possible score.

14 Building the Right Strategy for You

Know your strengths and play to them

I see an awful lot of amateur golfers who really have worked hard and developed pretty good golf swings. I do not mean that they are technically sound enough to join the pro tour, but they are capable of hitting a steady stream of solid, fairly straight shots, and they are respectable putters to boot. Watching them on the practice tee, you would expect them to break 80 consistently. Yet it never ceases to amaze me that they almost always fail to do so. Not only that, an alarming percentage of the time they sky all the way into the 90s!

For golfers whose skills are not quite that high, the difference between what they should score and what they do score is even more pronounced. I am talking about the golfer who should shoot no worse than 90. To do that, all the player needs to do is bogey every hole on a par 72 course; with some decent planning he is very capable of that. In fact, he can hit several greens in regulation and make a half-dozen pars per round, so shooting 90 should be a breeze. This golfer should be thinking 85 every time out. Instead, he is susceptible to several horrible holes each and every round, which launch his score up to the 100 range.

Why does this type of disaster occur so often at all levels of amateur play? Believe it or not, it happens because most amateurs' *strategy* skills need more tuning than their ball-striking abilities! They neither understand nor play to their strengths and weaknesses. They do not realize that certain course conditions limit them to certain types of shots. When in trouble, they attempt miracle recovery shots out of fierce rough, under trees or over water that would make a young Arnold Palmer blanch! They do not know when to cut their losses or accept that it is OK to humbly accept a bogey now and then.

In short, these golfers are not sound, fundamental strategists. And strategy is important. I would go so far as to say that you will improve your score as much by applying consistently solid strategy to your game based on your individual skill level as you will from the swing improvements you have gained from the previous chapters.

Below I explain all the points you must consider in playing shots from the tee, the fairway, from the rough and around and on the greens. Chances are you overlook many factors that would help you to approach a shot as you should. So let's do a little "consciousness-raising" and study these factors.

What do you think about when you stand on the tee of a par 4 or par 5 hole? You have two major considerations and a number of secondary ones. The first you should ask is, "What is the best position from which to play my second shot?" The second is, "What is the major problem area that I must avoid from the tee?"

Most amateurs automatically assume that the best place they can be is in the middle of the fairway, as far out as they possibly can drive the ball. I agree that if your tee shot is lying right on the "pipeline" you are rarely in bad position. However, that second element—trying to hit the ball as far as you can— practically guarantees that you *will not* hit it down the middle.

Accuracy means much more than distance in driving. You should try to place your tee shots just as accurately as if you were hitting a short iron to the pin. Do you swing from your heels on a 130-yard 8-iron shot? Of course not, and you should not with the driver either. Think of hitting the shot solidly, not hard, and you will quickly see the gain in accuracy.

You can begin to refine your tee-shot planning by asking yourself, "What's the *best* spot on the fairway to hit my approach to?" As a general rule of thumb, you always want to have an approach to the flag that is unimpeded by a hazard and that gives you the most open green to aim at. If the pin is tucked on the left side of the green with bunkers on both sides, you should try to hit your tee shot to the right side of the fairway, and vice versa.

Another point to consider is the width of the fairway. Today, many courses feature "contoured" fairways, meaning that they are wider at some points than others. Sometimes it makes sense to hit your tee shot a little less than your maximum distance in order to give you more fairway to aim at.

Let's say you are playing a 375-yard par 4, and you can hit a solid tee shot 240 yards. This drive would leave you a short iron to the green, so you get up and smash away with your driver. However, at the 240-yard mark the fairway becomes a narrow neck between two fairway bunkers—a tough target for anyone to hit. If you take out your 3-wood and hit a 225-yard shot instead, you will have almost twice as much fairway to hit. Plus, if you hit it a little off-line, you will come up just short of the bunkers.

On a hole like this, it pays to give up a little yardage for safety. If your 3-wood shot comes off as planned, you will have a relatively easy 150-yard shot from the fairway. And I might add that, by thinking out your tee-shot strategy beforehand, you are much more likely to execute confidently and correctly than if you were to swing away with the driver at that narrow target. Subconsciously, you will *know* that the odds of hitting the fairway are not good.

Now, don't get me wrong. There are times when you have to go with the driver. Suppose you were playing to the same tee shot area, but the hole was 440 yards long. If you were to lay up, you could not get home in two anyway, so the long drive is worth the risk.

Let's not forget our second major point on tee-shot strategy: avoid the major problem areas that the hole presents. Sometimes this danger factor allows you to aim in the same direction as does your desire to set up an easy second shot. And sometimes it forces you to decide between optimum position and safety.

In the example of the hole with the pin tucked on the left, we said we wanted to drive the ball to the right side of the fairway. Let's suppose that this hole also had an out of bounds or a water hazard to the left of the fairway. Even more reason to keep the ball right—no problem there. But what if the out of bounds or water is on the right? Do you still try to hit the right side of the fairway in search of the easy approach shot or do you play your tee shot left, away from trouble, leaving yourself a tougher angle for the approach shot?

Here is where your strategy varies depending on the strengths and weaknesses in your game. Are you a confident wood player, sure that you can put the ball in the landing area that will leave you that open approach? If so, go for it. However, if you are not that confident in your driving but feel you are a steady iron player, it makes sense to play the safe line off the tee and accept a slightly tougher second shot. In most cases, this is the sounder strategy. After all, if you gamble and lose with water or out of bounds, you lose either one or two full strokes. If you are a little too much on the safe side, you can still put it on the green and make your par.

Always weigh the severity of the hazards you are dealing with. If you have only light rough on either side to worry about, you can pretty much play for the best position for a good shot at the flag because there is no severe penalty for a miss.

By the way, whenever you decide to aim for one side of the fairway or the other, you will get a better perspective on your target by teeing it up on the opposite side of the tee from the side of the fairway you want to hit. Aim right, tee left.

Dogleg holes can also present tantalizing strategic choices. It is always a thrill when you successfully cut the corner over tall trees or a nest of bunkers, leaving you a much shorter approach shot. But there are dangers. I am not telling you never to try to cut corners off the tee, but I do think you should weigh the benefits against the penalties.

Let's say the dogleg hole is a relatively short par 5. If you play it straight down the fairway you will need three shots to get home; cutting the corner successfully will give you a chance to get home in two. Then it might be worth a try. But if the hole is a medium to short par four, cutting corners just is not worth it. If you are successful your reward might be a wedge to the green, but if you drive it down the middle you will probably have no more than a 7-iron anyway. In this case I would say play it by the book and let the others flirt with possible disaster.

One last point on tee shots on doglegs: if you decide to cut corners, make sure that you do it only on holes that bend in the same direction as your natural shape of shot. If you draw the ball consistently, do not try to "take it over the top" on a hole that bends sharply right. It just is not worth the risk.

Let's move on to the proper strategic decisions on your approach shots to the greens, both when you have put your drive in Position A, the perfect position to attack the flag on your approach, and when you have found some other locations—as we all do more often than we would like.

Let's tackle Position A considerations first. You are on the fariway with a clear line to the pin. It looks like you can go right at it. But before you do, ask youself these questions. Are there any hazards fairly close by if you should happen to miss the shot? Is most of the trouble short of the green or behind it? Will the ball hold where it lands or should you plan for some run? How comfortable are you with the club you need for the distance? Is your lie good enough so you are sure of how the ball will fly? What is the best angle to putt from on this green?

If you feel comfortable about the shot and have no severe hazards to worry about, by all means, fire at the flag. One small caution, though: you will almost always leave yourself an easier putt if your shot finishes a little short of or below the hole; and if you should miss the green just short, it is usually easier to get the ball up and down from there than it is when you "airmail" it over the green.

On par 3 tee shots, you are really in Position A to begin with. You can tee the ball anywhere within the teeing area that improves your angle to the pin, and you can even move the ball back from the tee markers up to two club lengths, making it easier to hit the shot the correct distance. Use these advantages and always tee up your ball as well.

But you will often find yourself somewhere other than Position A. Here is where the good strategies make the right decisions and the bad the wrong ones.

Let's start with situations where you have a shot to the green, but a difficult one. You may be on the wrong side of the fairway so that your path to the pin is blocked, in the rough or both. The first question to ask yourself is, "What combination of shots is likely to get my ball into the hole in the fewest shots from this point?" Maybe iron play is really your forte and you are confident that you can go directly at the pin successfully. If so, fine. But you may think the better plan is to aim for the open side of the green or the largest area of the green, even if it leaves you a longer putt. If you are a good long putter, it makes sense to play to the fat of the green, particularly when your lie is less than perfect. If you are hitting from rough, you have to allow some room for the ball to run when it lands anyway. And the longer the club you are hitting from one of these less-than-perfect angles, the more it makes sense to follow this "get it on the green" philosophy. You have still got an excellent chance to make your par, and occasionally you will get a bonus and drop a long one for birdie.

An integral part of strategy is to determine what to do when you are really in trouble—deep in the trees, buried in heavy rough or in a fairway bunker with a steep lip. Oftentimes you will be tempted to say to yourself as you survey one of these predicaments, "I can get it on the green if I hit the shot just perfectly." And you are right, you probably can. But if you had to try the shot ten times, how many times would you actually put it on the green. Twice? Three times? If so, it is probably not worth the gamble. Keep in mind the realities should you miss. If the ball is likely to hit a tree and ricochet into deep woods or out of bounds, or if you risk burying a long iron from a fairway bunker into its wall in front of you, play it smart. Pitch through a wider opening in the trees to a point in front of the green. Use a more lofted iron to get safely out of the bunker, even if you cannot get home.

Many amateurs believe that any time they are forced to play for a bogey, they are being cowardly or somehow not "giving it all they've got." Hogwash. You are still adhering to the fundamental philosophy of taking the lowest possible number of strokes *from the position you are now in*. Believe me, the pros realize that, when they are in a bind, making bogey is not too bad. That is one reason they are pros!

Every now and then, you will wind up saving par after playing the intelligent recovery by making a good pitch and one putt. Do this enough times and you will know you have the right approach.

Let's talk now about your strategy in the short game, for those times in a round when you have either missed the green with your approach or had to play safe because your tee shot found trouble. You may also be in the happy position of being close to the green on a par 5 in two strokes.

In playing short-game shots you will usually be focusing on getting the ball as close to the hole (or in it) as possible. Of course, you will encounter lies and pin positions that make it almost impossible to get close, from where you may have to stick with that "fat of the green" philosophy that you often use on full approaches. More often, though, you will be looking at short pitch shots, chips and bunker shots that you want to get as close to the hole as possible to virtually assure that one-putt par. So, whereas your strategy might lean a little toward the conservative side from the tee or on the fairway, I would be happy if I helped you become a more aggressive short-game palyer. Try to hole it!

Really, club selection is the most important part of short-game strategy, assuming that you are going for the hole with your shot. I see amateurs make terrible mistakes in the area of club selection, making it tougher than it should be to get the ball close. Often, a player relies on a favorite "chipping" club to play all of his or her short shots. This is faulty strategy. There are about seven clubs—say, the 6-iron through the sand wedge, plus the putter—that can make your recovery infinitely easier when you pick the right club for the right shot. When you have a good lie and little green to work with, go with the sand wedge. Other times, you may be just off the green where a low, running chip with a 6-iron will be much easier to judge. In general, it is good strategy to "use" the green you have available between you and the hole, landing the ball on the green for the truest possible bounce and letting it run from there. I will say more on this strategy in the upcoming chapters on the short game.

There is strategy in putting, too. You might think that your object is simply to hole every putt—this almost always holds true on shorter putts, but you will run into situations, particularly on fast or sloping greens, where it is smart to plan on leaving yourself the easiest possible second putt should your first one miss. Usually, in these situations you shoud try to leave yourself a straight putt that is either flat or uphill.

Another part of being a good putting strategist is to pay close attention to the speed of your longer putts, because if you hit all your putts the right length you will rarely have a long second putt. Of course, I will go into more detail on putting mechanics as well as planning in chapter 18.

I hope by now you are convinced that there is much more to improving your total golf game than learning a better swing. You can save as many or more strokes just by applying sound, fundamental strategic decisions to every stroke you play from tee to cup. I suggest that you think about these points on every shot you play the next time out. You will probably notice that your usual shot-making strategy is quite a bit different from the thoughts outlined here. If so, why not reread this chapter?

Part 4
The Short Game:
Long on Importance

15 Become a Wedge Master

Compact and firm beats long and lazy

The next three chapters deal with that elusive aspect of golf called the short game, otherwise referred to as "getting it up and down." This is the area of the game that the real players excel at—getting it up and down for birdie on the par 5s and saving par on the par 3s and 4s.

This might surprise you, but the greatest players in the world rarely, if ever, hit all eighteen greens in regulation during a round. In recent years the leader on the PGA Tour in the Greens in Regulation category has won that title while hitting about 70 percent of the greens, or about thirteen greens per round. The most accurate player on the Tour still has to get the ball up and down five times per round just to save par!

If the short game has that much significance to the pros, it has even more for you, because on average you will hit a lot fewer greens than they do, even if the courses you play are not as difficult. So you will face a lot more of these short-game or recovery shots. Naturally, the closer you get them to the hole, the easier it is to get them down in one putt.

Aside from putting, the short game breaks down into three segments: pitch shots in which you loft the ball over rough or hazards and carry the ball most of the way to the hole; bunker shots of all kinds; and chip shots designed to land the ball just on the putting surface so they run all the way to the hole. Let's look at the fundamentals, mechanics and techniques needed to execute each of these shots and the variations within each category.

The one thing I cannot teach you that each of you who read this must learn on an individual basis, is the perception of what type of short-game shot to hit in any situation and the feel and sensitivity with which to execute the one that is needed. You achieve this through practice, trial and error, observing what works and remembering it so that you can make the right choice next time out on the course. In actual play you must be able to perceive the shot you need to hit, then make a practice swing while mentally visualizing how your body will move in order to produce the contact and flight pattern desired. When you feel you have a clear picture of the motion, you then step up and hit the shot.

This chapter deals with pitching. I define a pitch shot as any approach from 60 to 90 yards out (depending on the strength of the player) on in to no less than 5 yards off the edge of the green. So I am referring to shots that are less than full shots, ones for which you want to fly the ball most or all the way to the hole. You will be using your sand wedge, pitching wedge or possibly your 9-iron when hitting this shot.

Successful pitching, as part of the short game, relies heavily on feel and sensitivity coupled with good fundamentals. I repeat: the number-one axiom of the fundamental approach is that "the setup predetermines the motion." Your setup for hitting pitch shots is one in which you want to restrict or reduce your overall freedom of movement. The number-one problem most golfers must overcome in hitting a good pitch shot is *overswinging*. So let's gear our pitching fundamentals to help eliminate or at least reduce this tendency.

Hitting good pitch shots requires maximum feel with minimum movement. Your purpose in setting up is to place your body in what I call a receptive position, that is, the pitching swing is mainly an arm swing. (See figure 27.) The shoulders and hips will turn, and lower-body weight will shift only as much as the arms swing enough to cause this to happen. In other words, keep your body passive and submissive to the swinging of your arms.

You probably want to ask, "How much should my arms swing?" This is the million-dollar question, but there are no axioms or absolutes or laws that dictate the answer. Even given a standard length of pitch shot, the extent to which your arms swing is a variable that differs with each and every golfer because we all differ in our physical strength and the amount of clubhead speed we generate. Our hands and arms must be at their maximum sensitivity and our bodies at their maximum responsiveness. First you must decide on the type of shot you must hit. Second, you must take a practice swing, evaluating and calculating the amount of grip and muscle pressure, length of swing and level of power you must impart at impact to produce the desired shot.

You might find yourself adjusting your estimates of how much swing you will need for a given shot. For example, on your first practice swing your mental picture of the motion might have you saying to yourself, "That's too much swing." So you take another practice swing that is a little less forceful—maybe then you say to yourself, "That's not enough swing." Your third practice swing will be somewhere between the first two. When you get the correct motion, your inner response will be, "That's it, now execute with that exact swing length, muscle tone and power level." This preshot research is a necessary ingredient in developing the feel that must be present for you to successfully execute accurate pitch shots. The preshot research affects and dictates what your setup fundamentals will be. The more you play these shots and really think about the

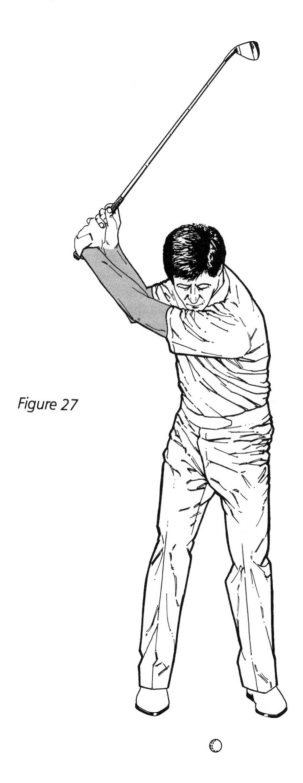

Figure 27

amount of swing you need, incidentally, the more you will find that you have the right "feel" for the shot on your first practice swing. You will need to adjust less and less and you will not be holding up play either!

Since the pitch shot requires a smaller swing than a full shot does, you need to set up in a postion that will effectively reduce the arc of your swing. As I said earlier, the number-one error golfers make in hitting pitch shots is overswinging. Overswinging builds up too much power and motion for the shot at hand. When your mind senses this buildup, there is only one correction you can make—you decelerate, reduce power, bail out and try to slow down the speed of the clubhead. This bailout has one of three results: 1) a relatively decent shot; 2) a skulled shot; or 3) a fat shot, also known as a "chunk" or a "chili-dip." Let me explain how the two flawed shots come about. The skull results from muscle tension increasing as you try to stop, slow down or hold back the speed of the club in the downswing. This muscle tension causes contraction of the muscles and a subsequent raising up of the body, so that the leading edge of the club hits the ball at its center or even above it. The deceleration of the hands in the downswing also stops them from squaring up the clubface at impact, so that you push the ball to the right of the target or perhaps even shank it.

The fat shot occurs when the golfer holds back as he begins the downswing but then lets go or tries to accelerate again at the last instant before impact. Then the muscles stretch again and the player lunges down at the ball, so that he sticks the club in the ground before it hits the ball. In both of these missed wedge shots, the problem is overswinging. Your swing must be consistently paced from start to finish, with the club accelerating through the ball at impact.

I would say that 99 percent of the golfers I work with take too wide a stance for their pitch shots. If a player's normal pitching wedge shot goes 100 yards, but he faces a 60-yard shot, usually he will set up just as he would for the 100-yard shot. Somewhere between the top of the backswing and the ball, he must back off the shot. This is harmful. I firmly believe that every shot from driver to putter (including pitch shots) should be hit with an accelerating action through impact.

A narrower stance is vital because it effectively reduces body motion and weight shift during your pitching swing. If your arms swing too far, your body will respond with a shoulder-turn so that your weight shifts too far over onto your right foot, causing a loss of balance. The narrower stance is essential to a sense of balance. Since the pitch shot is a partial or "little" shot, you must set up to hit it with a "little" or narrow stance.

Your stance should also be open, that is, your left foot should be drawn back from the aiming line. Your weight distribution should slightly favor the left side; the degree will vary depending on the length and height of the shot you intend. These two basics allow for a smooth and free arm swing and weight transfer to your left side down and through the ball and into the finish.

The second variable that helps you control distance on your pitch shots is over-swing. How much to choke up is an individual preference that you can only learn through practice. Generally, the shorter the shot, the more you should choke up on the club. The combination of narrower stance and shorter club means less swing, more control, acceleration at impact, crisp contact and a better shot.

On pitch shots I ask golfers to think and feel as though the swing is a pendulum. Remember that for every action there is an equal and opposite reaction. A backswing in which the clubhead's arc is *x* length should produce a follow-through arc that is also of *x* length. It is easier to maintain constant muscle tone, pressure and power level when your swing is of equal length in both directions. Remember, the pitch shot is primarily an arm and hand swing. Your body motion, your turn and your weight shift remain passive and submissive to the motion of your arms. In fact, you should feel that your hands and wrists are even somewhat submissive in that they rotate only as dictated by the length of your arm swing.

Another point for you to remember is that the greater the loft on the club, the greater the force you will need to hit the ball a given distance. I prefer and recommend that you use the least lofted club possible for the shot while still hitting the ball high enough for it to land comfortably on the green and run to the hole from there. This approach demands a shorter swing. I believe that less swing means less chance for error. Since you always want to reduce your margin of error, use less loft and make a shorter swing. Again, practice to develop feel—that will dictate what the best shot is and how to execute it.

Most good players hit their best pitch shots when they try to carry the ball to an interim target or landing spot. I recommend that, whenever possible, this spot should be on the green itself because then you have the best chance to gauge the amount and direction of bounce and roll accurately. When you hit into the fringe, the ball may bounce off line to the right or left or take an extra-long bounce or, conversely, pull up dead. So for the best, most consistent results, land the ball on the green whenever you can.

Let's talk about a few special pitch-shot refinements to put in your pitching arsenal. The first is the "knockdown" pitch shot, used when you want to keep your pitch lower than normal. Because the trajectory is lower, the ball will naturally run more, although it will be "grabbing" into the green with each skip it takes. Use this shot when the pin is toward the back and you have plenty of green on which to run the ball. This shot is especially useful when the wind is in your face. And remember that you can hit this shot with your short or middle irons as well as with the wedges.

For the knockdown pitch, set up with a narrow stance. Depending on the length of the shot, the insides of your heels may be anywhere from a few inches to twelve to sixteen inches apart. Place 60 to 80 percent of your weight on your left side. Again, this will vary depending on the length of the shot. The shorter the pitch, the more weight you put on your left. Practice to find the optimum weight distribution for various shots.

Play the ball in the center of your stance or maybe even slightly right of center. Your stance should be open, although your hips and shoulders should remain square. Keeping the upper body square to the target line will help you return the club more squarely to impact and keep the follow-through low. On the knock-down pitch in particular, you want to avoid any outside-in cutting action that will pop the ball up.

One problem that many amateurs have with the knockdown pitch is their failure to release their hands. Releasing the hands at impact squares up and may even close the clubface slightly at impact, delofting the club and thus effectively keeping the ball down. The amount of release you use is again personal. You must practice and get a feel for it, so you can decide how much to release, and then execute. Remember that releasing your hands may cause a slight draw, so you may need to adjust your aiming line to the right for the amount of draw you expect.

Another shot that you must have in your bag if you want to be a complete player is the high soft lob shot, which I sometimes refer to as the *pancake pitch*. This is a pitch shot to use when you need to make the ball sit down quickly. Use this shot when the pin is tucked tightly behind a bunker, heavy rough or water that you must carry.

The key to this shot is knowing how to get as much height on the shot as you can. So play it with your sand wedge; if you happen to carry three wedges, as a fair number of players do, this situation is when that lofted third wedge makes the shot a lot easier.

Set up with a narrow stance. Your weight should be neutral or centered between the feet. Play the ball in the center of your stance or a couple of inches left of center. Lay the clubface back as much as you need to give it extra loft, so you can hit the shot as high as you need to. Remember that when you lay the face back it must still point squarely at the target. Also keep in mind that you should only play this shot from a good lie. You can easily skull the shot if the lie is tight.

Your stance should be open in relation to the target line so you can make a more upright backswing than normal. The more height you need, the more you should let your wrists cock as your club moves to the top of the backswing.

In the downswing, your hands should move freely enough to square up the clubface at impact. However, they cannot release full or else you will lose some of that loft you must have for this shot. As you can see, this is definitely a "feel" shot, and the more you can practice, the better you will time the hand action I have just described. You may want to feel that you are actually cutting across the line of flight a little, as if you are popping or scooping the ball up. The more you slide the club under the ball and the more the ball rolls up the clubface, the more height and backspin the shot will have. I like to imagine that the ball will land with a sort of "splat"; in reality, it will roll just a little, but not much.

The success of this shot depends on accelerating the clubhead under and through the ball and into a full finish. You must not be timid, scared or hesitant at impact. You must have guts to swing aggressively while sliding the club under the ball.

The third special pitch that every golfer needs to play often is the pitch shot from rough. Your setup will be the same as for the pancake pitch, except for a few alterations. First, tighten your forearms and wrists slightly at address. This will reduce the tendency of the taller grass to grab the clubhead and twist it, usually closing the clubface and causing an off-line shot to the left. Next, choke up on the grip by about two inches. This will help prevent the grass grabbing your club in the backswing. If the grass is long enough, you may also have to cock or lift the club more quickly on the backswing and bring it down on the same steep path. This will help keep grass from getting between the clubface and the ball at impact, which can rob you of control.

You may have to work hard and maybe even force your follow-through if the grass is very long and thick. The firmness in your arms and wrists will help you keep the clubface square at impact and the ball more truly on line to the hole.

In your preswing routine, you first have to decide how much the ball will be slowed by the grass. Then determine your setup, degree of muscle tension at address and the power level you will apply to your swing.

This completes our discussion of pitching, which is the "long-range" segment of the short game. Let's move in a little closer to the green now and sharpen your chipping game.

16 You Can Be a Better Chipper

Make your chips roll like putts

To me, chipping is one of the most enjoyable aspects of the game of golf. Nestling those little running shots from around the green "dead" to the hole (or in it!) is the essence of maximizing your score. In reality, becoming a good chipper is as much dependent on accurate visualization and planning of the shot as it is on the quality of your execution. Chipping is easy when you know exactly what shot you need to play.

Chip shots consist of those very short strokes made from just inches to a maximum distance of 5 yards off the green. The ball might be resting on the first cut of fringe or in the light rough just beyond. While the mechanics of chipping are pretty simple, the shot can call for a variety of clubs—anything from a sand wedge down to a 5-iron, depending on how far you are off the green, the distance to the pin, the slope and speed of the green and other factors.

Like pitching, successful chipping relies heavily on feel and sensitivity and a preswing routine. However, there are a couple of axioms that you should always use to guide your planning of any chip shot.

First, always examine the shot to see if you can putt instead of chip. That is, determine whether the ground between your ball and the green is smooth enough to allow you to use a putter without a ball bouncing erratically. Believe me, you will almost always putt the ball closer to the cup than you can chip it. Or, negatively speaking, a bad putt will usually wind up a lot closer than a bad chip. You have a greater margin of error if you can putt the ball.

When should you chip? You must look closely at the area between your ball and the green before making that decision. Consider putting if the grass height is consistent, pretty short and either growing straight up or leaning in the direction you will be rolling the ball. Bare spots with a ridge, clumps of extra thick or long grass, weeds, or grass growing and leaning toward you are variables that demand that you chip over them rather than putt through them. You must chip in these instances because you cannot even remotely predict how the ball will roll through and come out onto the green, either in terms of speed or direction.

My second axiom regarding chip shots is that you should strive to make them roll like putts as much as possible. It is always easier to judge distance to the hole in terms of roll than in terms of flight. Therefore, use the least lofted club that will still loft the ball onto the putting surface and let it roll the rest of the way to the hole. We hit more putts than any other shot in golf, so making your chips like your putts will sharpen your visualization of the shot.

What about the area of club selection for chips shots that I mentioned earlier? Well, there are two schools of thought on club selection for chipping (you can probably guess which side I favor already). One school advises you to use the same club for all chips, reasoning that if you use only one club you will become better at handling it in different ways. There is some truth to this theory, and as great a golfer as Seve Ballesteros developed his skills by playing all kinds of shots with one club while he was growing up.

The second school suggests using different clubs, depending on the shot at hand. Believers in this method say you should select and use the club that provides the amount of loft you need to carry the ball onto the green and then roll it the desired distance to the hole. I agree with this theory 100 percent. Use the proper club for the job at hand. I do not buy the idea that using the same club makes you a more adept chipper, because, although the club is the same, each shot is different and thus must be hit differently. Using only one club for chipping merely makes the job harder than it should be.

The problems of chipping are basically the same as those you encounter playing pitch shots. Overswinging or failing to get enough loft when chipping both cause tensing of muscles and deceleration of the clubhead. The result of these flaws can be skulling, or what we know as the fat shot, the chunk or the chilidip. Of the two problems, my experience has been that the bigger one for most golfers is too little loft. They try to manipulate the ball by scooping it up in the air and usually end up with a skulled chip that runs way past the hole.

For a better idea of the club selection you should make for any given shot, study the chart below. It tells you how much air-time and roll you can expect with various clubs, assuming that you are chipping to a fairly flat, medium-speed green.

Club	Air-time	Roll
Sand Wedge	7/8	1/8
Pitching Wedge	3/4	1/4
9-iron	5/8	3/8
8-iron	1/2	1/2
7-iron	3/8	5/8
6-iron	1/4	3/4
5-iron	1/8	7/8

Keep in mind that these are just approximations. You may get a little more air-time or roll on your chip shots depending on how you address the ball, how steep your clubhead descends on the ball and so on.

The first line on the chart applies to shots where you have just missed the green and the hole is close to the edge of the green; a total distance of, say, 15 to 25 feet from you. Since there is not much room for the ball to roll, you should use the lofted sand wedge or pitching wedge. On the other hand, if your are on the right fringe and the pin is on the very left of the green, about 85 feet away, say, you have the whole green to roll the ball across. So a 5-, 6- or 7-iron is the club to use.

The slope of the green, the direction of the grain and the speed of the green are all variables that affect your club selection. Chipping downhill, downgrain (with the grain) or on a really fast green dictates that you use one or two "less" clubs than you would for that distance if the ground were level and the green of normal speed. That is, you should use an 8- or 9-iron instead of a 7-iron. Conversely, chipping uphill, into the grain and on heavy or slow greens dictates less loft. Using a 7-iron instead of an 8- or 9- provides more force and more roll to combat the fact that the ball is running uphill and against the grain.

As you look for these factors, you will see that often they balance off against one another. For example, say you have a chip from a total distance to the pin (and a distance from your ball to the edge of the green) that would call for a 9-iron on a flat, medium-speed surface. The chip is uphill but with the grain and over a fast surface. All things considered, the 9-iron will probably still be the right club. Naturally, you must make these evaluations correctly in your preswing examination of the situation and determine the shot you need to hit and the club to use. Your practice swings will cue your muscle tone, power level and length of swing to produce the desired shot.

My second axiom, that chips should roll as much like putts as possible, implies that you must read the green beforehand, as if the shot were a putt, to determine the line and length on which the chip must roll for the ball to go to the hole. As on a pitch shot, you must pick an exact landing spot on the green. You base your intended line of roll on how you anticipate the direction of bounce the ball will have when it hits the green. Again, maximum roll is best when you can visualize it similarly to a putt. Since you hit more putts than any other shot in golf, your visualization will be better and your execution will improve.

How do you execute the chip shot correctly every time? Assume a stance that is open and extermely narrow. Your heels should be almost touching. Although the stance is open, your upper body should remain square to the line of flight. Your weight should favor your left foot, 60 to 70 percent on that side.

Place your hands ahead of the ball at address. Doing so presets an angle of attack that produces a slightly descending blow on the ball, so that you pinch or

Figure 28

nip the ball off the fringe. When you set up in this manner, your arms and club will form a sort of lower-case *y* at address.

Align the leading edge of your clubface square to the line of flight of the chip. *Do not* line it up at the hole automatically—remember that you must plan for the break on a chip shot just as you would on a long putt.

As for the pitch shot, execute an arm swing in which any body motion is simply a reaction to the swinging of your arms. Keep your body very still and passive throughout the stroke. You must maintain the *y* formed by your arms and the clubshaft at address throughout the swing, with your hands always leading the clubface and your left wrist never breaking down. I find that firming up the tricep muscles of your left arm at address (the muscles behind your upper arm) will help you achieve and maintain this firmness.

For most amateurs breaking the wrists is the number-one problem in chipping. When the left wrist breaks down, the clubhead catches up to or even passes the hands before impact, so that the ball is either skulled way past the hole or scooped up so that it finishes way short. This type of breakdown is what caused the infamous "double hit" by T.C. Chen in the 1985 U.S. Open.

To combat this fault, I suggest the following exercise. Take an old 7-iron and cut off the cap of the grip. Then take a shaft and insert it down the end of the club so that it protrudes about a foot beyond where you assume your grip (see figure 28).

Now when you execute the chip, if you keep your *y* intact, with your wrists firm and hands leading, the shaft will remain against your left forearm and never touch your left side. On the other hand, if you break your wrists, the shaft extension will swing back towards you and slap you on the left side of your rib cage. So this exercise provides instant feedback, leaving no doubt as to the correctness of your chipping stroke.

Practice chipping with the shaft extension until you can hit chip after chip and never "slap" yourself. Then, when you chip without the extension, imagine that it is still there and chip as though it is. Some people may call this exercise a gimmick. I agree, it is a mental and physical gimmick, but it works for me and I am sure it will improve your chipping too.

Remember to hit your chip shots with an arm and shoulder motion, maintaining the lower-case *y* with no wrist action. Keep your body submissive to the swinging of your arms and shoulders. Pick the right club to loft the ball onto the green and land it on your target spot, then let it roll on your intended line to the hole like a putt. Try to spend at least a few minutes practicing these things every time you are at the golf course. In no time you will find yourself saving that odd stroke here and there that you somehow always missed out on before.

17 Secrets of Sand Play

Take out the trauma—it's the easiest shot in golf

It is time to begin our examination of the greenside bunker shot, probably the most feared and most mishit shot in golf. It is incredible how many golfers' hearts begin to palpitate and how many begin to sweat bullets when their ball goes into a bunker. This type of golfer enters the bunker with the goal of merely getting the ball out in one shot. I do not mean on the green and close to the hole—he simply prays he gets the ball out, keeping it in play close to the green.

It is a shame that anyone is so scared of what is really a simple shot to execute. Believe it or not, you have a greater margin for error on the sand shot than on any fairway shot. Assuming you have a reasonable lie, you can "miss" this shot a little and still come up with fine results. More on that later. Hopefully, if you are one of those golfers who is seized by *trap trauma,* reading this chapter will put you on the road to recovery. You *can* become proficient in bunker play!

Before I explain the setup and swing techniques, let's look at what a bunker shot is and what happens when you play it.

A bunker shot is unique. It is the only shot in golf in which the clubface itself does not actually contact the ball. How then does the ball fly out of the trap? Technically, the displacement of sand under the ball by the clubface lifts the ball out. It flies out because the club hits the sand behind the ball, goes down and under it, and forces the sand up. The sand itself is what lifts the ball out. The more sand between the club and the ball, the less backspin the ball will carry, so that it pops out shorter but rolls farther. The less sand you take, the more spin you put on the shot so it carries farther but rolls less. So you see, you can hit most bunker shots a bit "fat" or "thin" and still have them travel about the same total distance. This important point can be a great confidence-builder whenever you face a bunker shot.

So, rule number one to becoming a good bunker player is that you have to have guts! To successfully execute a greenside bunker shot you must first have the guts to swing firmly and hit the sand behind the ball.

Let's address what to do when playing a basic sand shot. I am referring to the times when you have a good lie in a greenside bunker, perhaps 30 to 50 feet from the hole. Assume an open stance with your feet, hips and shoulders aimed about 20 degrees left of the target. You should distribute your weight evenly on your feet or, if anything, on your left side. The width of your stance should be about the same as for the pitch shot—heels about twelve inches apart.

Align your clubface so that it is open to your body alignment, but keep it square to your target line to the hole. Place the ball in the center of your stance, or slightly left of center when you need to hit a softer shot with more height.

You should hold your hands in a relatively low position, creating an angle between your arms and the club of about 45 degrees. Position your hands even with the ball or slightly behind it, so that your left wrist is in a slightly cupped or concave position. Your grip pressure should be light, yet firm enough to be certain that impact with the sand will not twist the clubface at impact.

The $84,000 question for golfers who are bedeviled by sand shots is, "How deep and how much sand do I displace and how hard do I swing?" You must study the depth and density of the sand, then determine how much force you will need to displace the proper amount of sand for the desired shot. Remember that the texture of the sand can vary a great deal from course to course, and even from hole to hole on the same course. As you dig in your feet to play the shot (and you should always dig in a bit to assure that you do not slip during the swing), you will be able to determine how deep the sand is. The deeper the sand, the greater the degree of force you need to hit the ball the same distance as you would if the sand is thin.

Your swing for a bunker shot should be a long, lazy, slow and methodical one. It should be wristier than the swing for any tee or fairway shot. Thus, the arc of the clubhead is more of a U, the product of a very upright backswing followed by an abrupt and upright follow-through after impact. Some players describe the sensation of the follow-through as feeling as if they are pulling the club up to their chest, with their hands moving under the ball and releasing so they have the added feeling of scooping the ball out.

The divot or path through the sand that you cut out should be a fairly long and shallow one (see figure 29). For ordinary greenside shots, you should *not* try to dig the ball out. You slide it out or scoop it out. I cannot emphasize enough that you do not need to "muscle" the ball out on a normal bunker shot. You only need to make a big enough swing to create the clubhead speed you need so that the flange of your sand wedge cuts or slices into the sand and slides under the ball.

There is no substitute for the practice that will give you the experience you need to examine, perceive, visualize and execute with confidence.

It helps immensely if you can develop specific mental imagery for playing the basic sand shot. Why? If you can imagine the playing of the shot as a different

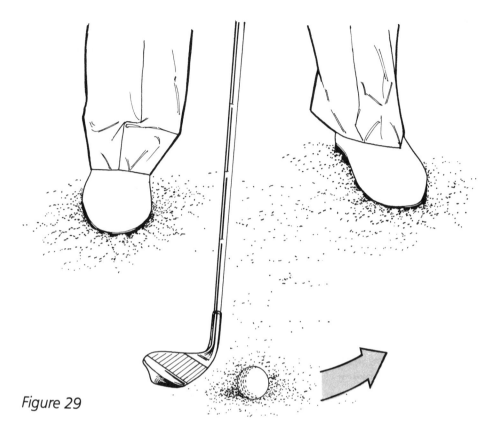

Figure 29

task, one that uses images not usually related to golf, you will begin to think of the shot as a routine sort of task instead of a terrifying situation.

In my lessons, I provide my students with examples I use or that other golfers have used successfully, as follows:

Image #1: Imagine that the ball is sitting on a giant cake of cheese. You are going to get the ball up and away by cutting a long thin slice out of the top of the cheese. The thinner and longer the slice, the faster the club slices under the ball. This quick slicing action creates backspin for stopping power. The deeper the slice you take, the shorter the distance the ball will fly, carrying less spin and running farther upon landing.

Image #2: Picture a perfectly round fried egg, about six to eight inches in diameter, with the yolk in the dead center. The yolk represents the ball. Your object in making the swing is to loft the entire egg out of the trap while not breaking the yolk. Visualize landing the egg on the green unbroken, yolk up, as you would do with a spatula when putting it on a plate. Make the club enter the sand at the back of the egg and come out at the front of it.

If you want to put a lot of backspin on the shot, as when the pin is tucked close to the bunker, imagine that you are extracting a bigger egg, but that you want to take a shallower slice underneath it. If you do not need a lot of backspin, as when the pin is farther away from you, imagine a smaller egg and take a deeper cut, narrowing the arch of the U that your clubhead describes during the swing.

Whether you try for a spinning shot (which admittedly demands a little more touch) or the deeper cut with less backspin, you must have the guts to stand in there and swing freely through the sand. I think "slice the sand" is the best phrase to help produce the imagery and execution for a successful shot.

While we are on the subject of imagery and phraseology, I should mention that I really disagree with the often-used description of any shot from a green-side bunker as an "explosion shot." To me, this conjures up a picture of the golfer muscling and digging the ball out with tremendous effort. This forcing action is only applicable when the ball is in a buried lie. "Slice the sand" conveys a much more appropriate image.

You might have noticed that in describing how to play the shot, I have not once stated that you should hit, say, two inches behind the ball, or any particular distance for that matter. There is no such absolute measurement for how far to hit behind the ball. Every sand shot is different. You have to feel the sand with your feet as you dig in and judge how far behind and how deep you should slice under the ball. You really should not worry if it is an inch and a half, two inches, two and a half inches or three inches. That distance is whatever it needs to be; it happens based on your intuitive judgment. I teach my students not to get caught up in deciding how far in inches the club should hit the sand behind the ball. I believe this makes them too intense, in effect "sand-bound," which also makes them very susceptible to digging into the sand. It takes the feel out of the shot and also takes the slicing instinct out of the swing. So, hit the sand by feel, not by inches.

Now let's move on to the more difficult buried-ball situation. When I say "buried," I mean that half to all of the ball is below the surface of the sand. This is the time when you have to think "dig," because that is the only way you will get the ball out.

Your stance for the buried lie should only be a tiny bit open, with your weight more definitely favoring the left side than for a normal bunker shot. Position the ball at the center of your stance or slightly back of it. The farther back you play the ball, the lower and more running the ball will come out. The main advantage of the ball-back position is that it *will* get the ball out.

Address the ball with your clubface square to slightly closed (see figure 30). The square-to-closed blade helps the leading edge of the club dig, whereas the open-faced wedge would glide through a shallow layer of sand—not deep enough to get under the ball.

Incidentally, when you face a ball that is really buried, you may want to consider playing the shot with a pitching wedge. Since the flange is much smaller

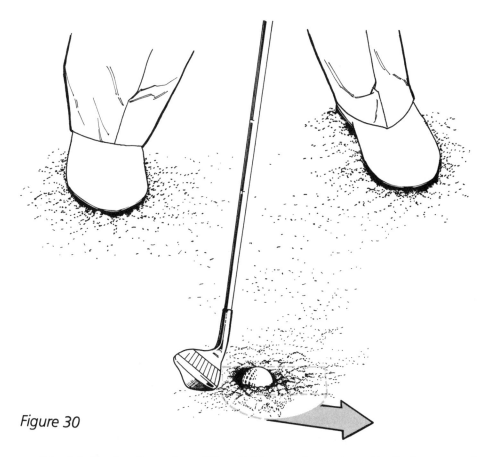

Figure 30

on this club, the leading edge of the pitching wedge automatically does a much better job of digging. Caution: you must be sure that you will clear the lip of the trap.

Grip the club more firmly than for the basic sand shot. This will help you resist the force of the sand. Try to visualize the length of swing and level of power you need to get the ball out, and what will happen once it lands.

For the buried lie, your swing should not be as wristy as for the normal bunker shot. In fact, the wrists should be as firm as for a regular tee or fairway shot. Take the club back to a three-quarter position with your wrists firm, then pull the club steeply down and into the sand with your left arm controlling the action. Remember that from a buried lie the ball will always come out low, ''hot,'' as experienced golfers say, and running. So be sure that your clubface alignment will provide enough loft to clear the bunker lip if there is one. You may have to adjust your body and club into a more open setup if you need height to clear a lip.

What about situations where the lie is such that the ball will probably run past the hole upon landing? You actually can reduce roll by restricting your follow-through. If the hole is close to the bunker, practice driving the club into the sand but leaving the clubhead there with no follow-through. When you do, the sand will not be displaced as forcibly and the ball will come out more softly. This shot might seem risky, but if you practice it a bit before using it on the course, you will see that it works. Remember, the higher the follow-through, the more sand you displace and the farther the ball will go. Sticking the club in the sand guarantees that the ball will not fly far. Be careful that your level of force and angle of attack are sufficient to pop the ball far enough to clear the lip of the trap.

What about a ball buried in the face of a bunker, near the lip? You must be careful in hitting this shot for two reasons: first, you can easily lose your balance and fall backwards into the trap due to the steep sidehill angle. Second, if you do not hit the ball with enough power or on a low enough angle to move the ball forward, it might hit the lip and pop back into the trap. Remember also that should this unfortunate result occur, the ball must not hit or touch you or your club. If it does you will be penalized two strokes according to Rule 19-2A and 2B of The United States Golf Association's Rules of Golf.

Another sand shot you will run into fairly frequently is the shot from a wet or bare spot in a bunker. You should think of the execution of this shot as the "ultimate slice." Your stance and clubface should be very open. Your swing should be very loose and wristy so that the U the clubhead describes will be very narrow. The divot will be rather short and very shallow. The club will slide under the ball very quickly. The slice you take will be clean, sharp and quick. While the overall swing is not at all fast, you should sense a quickness through impact. Because the club slides under the ball and your hands pull across the line and up and into your chest, you must visualize a super slicing action under the ball. You should feel and be more wristy on this shot than on any bunker shot, with your body stiller and more responsive to the swinging of your hands and arms.

Let's finish up this chapter with what is, I admit, a very challenging shot: the long greenside bunker shot. I define a "long" bunker shot as anything over 20 yards in length. It is a difficult shot because, in order to carry the distance, you must take less sand so that more force is applied to the ball. And the less sand you take, the riskier the shot is.

My first suggestion is to use a pitching wedge or 9-iron and hit a regular bunker shot. Since you are using less loft, you can still take some sand while carrying the needed distance. I think this is the safest way to play the shot.

Another alternative is to choke up on your sand wedge or pitching wedge and try to pick the ball cleanly off the sand. This shot is dangerous—a skulled or fat shot is likely, so you must have a great deal of confidence based on practice of the shot. Also, you must make sure there is very little or no lip since the ball will fly relatively low. Despite all this, it is a good shot to have in your bag because it increases your range for getting the ball to the hole on long bunker shots.

Whatever method you select, be aware of the following common problems in playing the long bunker shot, as well as ways to solve them:

1. Improper clubface alignment. Many golfers overdo the opening of the club-face. They may think that they must open the face automatically for any bunker shot, but with the club too open the ball will fly out to the right of the target and spin a little farther right upon landing. An overly open clubface also causes thin hits or outright skulls, but mainly, it is very difficult to get the ball all the way to the hole if you open the face. The important rule of thumb here is that no matter where your stance is pointing, the clubface must be square to the target, with the leading edge of the face perpendicular to your aiming or target line.

2. Swinging too fast and too hard. This problem usually causes the ball to fly out too far, over the green. The cure is a swing that is long, lazy and slow. Let your setup and square clubface do the job of propelling the ball forward.

3. Skulling the long bunker shot. This problem is caused by lifting the body, which in turn causes the club to miss the sand or get too little of it. You might skull the ball in to the lip of the bunker or line it out over the green. To cure this problem, you must stay level through the shot. Make a long, smooth swing, letting the club slice under the ball. Learn to trust your sand wedge. The club is as heavy as it is, and has a wide flange plus a great deal of loft—56 to 60 degrees—so that it will displace sand without digging and pop the ball up. So let it happen. Slide, slice or bounce the club under the ball and watch it pop out.

4. Not following through. Many players let the sand slow or stop the club upon impact. The result is obvious—the ball stays in the trap and you have to try again. The cure: visualize a follow-through during your preswing examination. You must trust that a full swing will produce a shot with the flight necessary to carry the ball close to the hole. Remember, the shape of the swing is a *U,* and after impact your hands come up and into the chest. On any long bunker shot, make sure that your follow-through is as long as your backswing.

We have covered a lot of ground on bunker play, so it may benefit you to reread this chapter. Then practice these tips and develop the feel sensitivity and experience that are musts for this area of play. This practice will enable you to visualize, sense, feel and finally execute with confidence. And, once you have done all the preparatory work, you must remember rule #1—dig in and have the guts to swing and displace sand. You will be amazed at the results. You might even ask yourself, "What was I ever so afraid of?"

18 Putting: The Game within a Game

Develop your own style

We have now covered all the shots you need to get your ball on the green and, we hope, close to the hole. Now let's look at how to get it in the hole.

Ben Hogan once said that golf is a two-faceted game—one part is played through the air and the other on the ground. Putting is where power, strength and length play second fiddle to touch, feel and sensitivity—and also courage. Putting is where you separate the tough from the timid. It is where a tap-in counts as much as a 250-yard drive. Putting, the "ground attack" if you will, is perhaps the most important, most talked-about, most written-about element of golf, yet it causes the greatest disappointment and frustration.

Putting accounts for at least 40 percent of your shots per round (varying slightly depending on how many shots it takes you on the average to reach all eighteen greens). If you take two putts per hole, you make thirty-six putts per round. Most amateurs will average between thirty-two and forty putts per round. *All* golfers should average under thirty-six. There will be several holes in each round where you will chip or pitch the ball very close to the hole so that you should definitely one-putt. And you should *never* three-putt more than one or two greens per round. If you average over thirty-six putts per round, you have an area where you can drastically cut strokes from your game.

I find it odd that most amateurs seem to assume that they are pretty much "stuck" with their putting as it is, for better or worse. Consequently, despite its importance, their putting remains neglected. These players hit balls on the practice range for hours yet never hit a single practice putt. Or if they do practice, it is only for a short time, usually while they are thinking about something else and not really working to improve.

My personal observations over the years lead me to conclude that high handicappers neglect their putting the most. That is a shame because they are the ones who have the greatest need for improvement. Just watch the putting green at your club some time. The players you see out there working on their putting are the better players. They know the value of a putt, how it will finish off that birdie for them or save that par.

The point here is to emphasize the importance of putting as a means of cutting strokes off your game. Intelligent practice will help you develop a stroke that is repetitive, that is, one that returns the putter to the ball squarely at impact, with the clubface pointing precisely where you aimed it at address. Practice will help you develop the feel, touch, sensitivity and perception to become a better putter. It is the one area of the game that everyone can improve, and I mean everyone. You may not be able to hit a drive 250 yards, but you can definitely sink a five-footer or even a fifty-footer.

Now that my little pep talk is over, let's study your putting setup. The putt is the one stroke that allows for your personal preference and feel in terms of posture, stance and grip. Although individual styles are more acceptable in putting than anywhere else, there are some good fundamentals that you should try to adhere to as well.

The width of your putting stance is entirely personal. However, I have noticed that the vast majority of good putters putt from a narrow stance—heels no more than eight inches apart. I believe that a relatively narrow stance gives your body maximum sensitivity for the stroke. It helps most golfers to stay still throughout the stroke as well. Note: when you are playing in windy conditions, it does help to widen your stance as much as feels comfortable to you. This will help anchor you should any gusts threaten to throw you off-balance.

As to your posture, I believe you should bend over at the waist slightly, standing relatively tall or erect, not crouched over. Let your arms swing so that you reduce any bending at the elbows or wrists. The fewer angles you have, the less chance that your stroke will break down. A relatively upright posture definitely contributes to greater firmness, less breaking of the wrists and thus more of a "pendulum" effect in the stroke itself (more on this later).

Your head should be perpendicular to your shoulders, not tilted one way or the other, with your eyes directly over the ball. Ideally, you could draw a straight line from your eyes to the ball, and another line at right angles to this line from your ball to the hole (see figure 31). It is okay if your eyes are slightly "inside" the line to the hole, but it is best to have your eyes directly over the ball and at right angles to your line of putt. This is crucially important because it affects your visualization and perception of the putt, thus it affects your feel, and ultimately your stroke.

If your head is tilted toward your right shoulder, for example, your eye-line will be aiming well to the right of the target. Your brain will "see" the hole as being farther to the left than it actually is, and you will most likely pull the putt. If your head is tilted to the left of your target line, your brain will see an image of the hole farther to the right, and you are likely to push or block the stroke. Remember, your muscles will react to what your brain senses, perceives and feels.

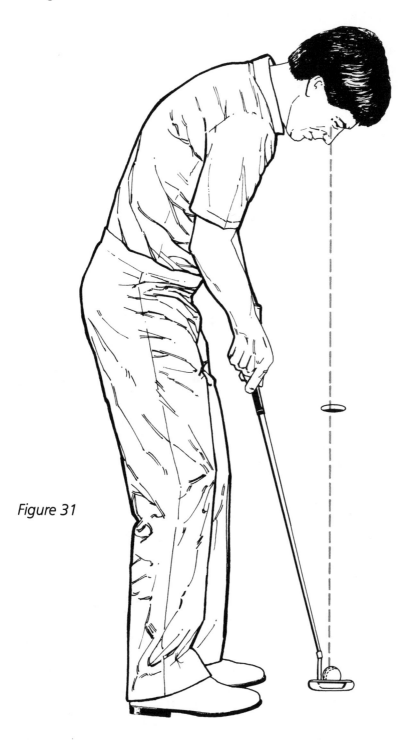

Figure 31

Where you have positioned your head and how you look at the hole creates the vision and the perception.

One last point on vision of the line of putt. When you look at the hole while standing over the ball, roll or swivel your head to the left so that your eyes move along the target line. This movement keeps your body level and passive. Many players tend to lift up their heads to look at the hole. This movement does not allow you accurate feedback for distance and slope and also lifts your body up out of your address position, so that you have to get back into posture and refigure the line before you putt. So, to minimize preswing motion, roll your head and watch your perception and feel improve.

You should position the ball opposite a spot just inside your left foot. With the pendulum-type stroke that I will discuss later, you will contact the ball at the very beginning of the upswing, giving the ball overspin so that it rolls end-over-end to the hole.

I suggest that you distribute your weight evenly or lean it a little more on your left side. You want to set your body in a position that will leave it passive yet receptive to the motion of the arms and shoulders.

How you grip the putter is your personal preference. However, there are some basics that I believe you should adhere to whatever grip you choose, as they provide maximum feel and consistent results in the stroke:

1. The hands should be facing each other so that they are palm to palm. Thus, they are opposing each other, adding firmness to the wrists and enhancing the sense of the hands working together as a unit.

2. Place both thumbs straight down the top of the grip. This position adds to your feel and to a one-piece action, as well as to the firmness of your wrists.

3. Keep your hands close together. This is another aid to feel and firmness— both hands working together as a unit.

The most commonly used putting grip is the reverse overlap. In this grip, the index finger of the left hand, pointing down, is placed over the fingers of the right hand. Many players use this grip because it firms up the muscles in the left wrist and reduces any tendency for the wrists to break.

I have even seen some golfers point their right index finger down the right side of the grip. They do this for the same reason—to develop firmness and to alleviate wrist-break. Many golfers claim added feel and confidence with this method. Finally, some golfers use the same grip to putt with that they use in their full swing. I think this is OK, provided your regular grip is a sound palm-to-palm grip.

The grip pressure that you use is again a personal preference. Find what is best for you by practice and by trial and error. Most teachers believe that, to provide maximum feel, your grip pressure should be soft. I agree, but I define it a bit more distinctly. The pressure should be soft, with no tension from the fingers to the elbows, yet with enough firmness to be in control. I like to think of the grip as being firm for a number of reasons. First, it helps reduce or eliminate wrist-break. Second, it adds power to the stroke for acceleration in the forward stroke and follow-through. A grip that is too soft makes you susceptible to decelerating the putter, which is the number-one reason putts are missed. This kind of putt makes you feel as if you hit a marshmallow, and the ball invariably comes up short. If you are consistently falling short of the hole, increase your grip pressure, make the same stroke and see if it doesn't help.

One last note on pressure. I believe you should increase your grip pressure as the putts get longer. Increased pressure with the longer stroke will add power, control, firmness and feel.

Let's talk now about the stroke itself. The overall motion of the putting stroke can be likened to the swinging of a pendulum. I believe that the motion originates from or is centered in the left shoulder-joint. The swinging of the shoulders will propel the arms, hands and club, all of which are somewhat passive and responsive to the swinging of the shoulders.

Many golfers get overly active with their hands and arms and end up with a wristy stroke because, paradoxically, they get bombarded with the axiom that "you must remain still in putting." Consequently, they freeze or lock their body but use all hands and arms to hit the ball. Generating your pendulum from your shoulders will create upper body motion and reduce hand action.

The key is to be sure that you do not sway or dip your head or shoulder. You can check this tendency by taking practice strokes in which you can see your shadow while watching your head. Your motion is correct if you see your shoulders move while your head remains still.

Here is another checkpoint that I find invaluable in keeping your stroke on track. At address the angle of your left elbow and wrist should not change during the entire stroke (see figure 32). This steadiness assures that your "pendulum" will have a constant arc, and that there will be no wrist-break during the stroke. The putter head should never pass the hands, except on very long putts. Maintaining your angles in this manner will also help you maintain balance and levelness of stroke.

During the stroke, you should try to keep the putter low to the ground, although of course the putter swings up just a little in both the backswing and the follow-through. Remember, the object is to develop a method that helps you swing the putter back and forth, returning the blade squarely into the back of the ball and square to the target line at impact. You must practice and experiment with all the variables discussed in this chapter to find the setup and motion that returns the putter to impact square to the target line, time after time.

What type of putter should you use? Like everything else in putting, this is a very personal choice. You need to find one with size, shape and weight to your liking. Liking what you look at adds confidence and definitely helps you make putts.

One of the biggest equipment errors I see golfers make is to select a putter

Figure 32

that is too long for them. If they hold it at its full length, they are forced to bend their arms at the elbows and wrists, creating too many angles that can go awry. The other danger when using a putter that is too long is choking up. This adjustment ruins the balance and weight distribution intended for that putter. If you choke up enough, the butt end of the putter can even wind up hitting you in the stomach! A putter is the right length when, if the golfer bends over, extends his arms and holds it at its end, the putter reaches the ground.

Grip size and style are important considerations. Thickness of the grip is again a personal preference, and you must decide for yourself which you like best, which feels best and which works best. There are many grip styles, and you have to test and decide what you like. Some grips have flat tops, which I think are great because they make it easy for you to put your thumbs down the shaft. Some bulge in the middle to provide more feel in the palms. Some players even use the same grip that is on the rest of their clubs. Work to find out what gives you the most confidence.

I would like to discuss one more point about putters that very few amateurs know about or understand even if they have heard about it. You must be able to identify the sweet spot on your putter and hit the ball with it on putt after putt. Tests have shown that missing the sweet spot by a single degree on a 30-foot putt will cause you to miss the hole by some fourteen inches.

Never trust the marking on a putter and assume that that is where the sweet spot is. Many are incorrect because the manufacturer places the line where it looks best cosmetically, or simply at the middle of the blade. Usually, the sweet spot is closer to the heel of the club. You can check your putter for its sweet spot by holding it between your thumb and index fingers (see figure 33). Lift it to where your head is nearly level with the clubface. With your other index finger, tap the face of the putter with a tee. When you hit the sweet spot, the putter-head will move straight back without twisting. When you find that spot, mark it or get a file and cut a line into the top of the clubhead.

Remember, putting style, from setup to grip to the putter itself, is a very personal aspect of the game. Following the basics and fundamentals outlined here will definitely make you a more consistent putter. Once you have developed your style and selected your putter, you must work at developing and maintaining your feel, sensitivity and motion.

By the way, if you feel your stroke is pretty good and the putts just do not seem to fall, I highly recommend that the first thing you should check on is your eyes. If your eyes are not working correctly, you certainly will not make as many putts as you would deserve to. Remember, you can have 20/20 vision but still have eye problems. Your depth perception may be off or you may have an astigmatism that affects your ability to align your clubface. The problems are many. Do yourself a favor and get your eyes checked.

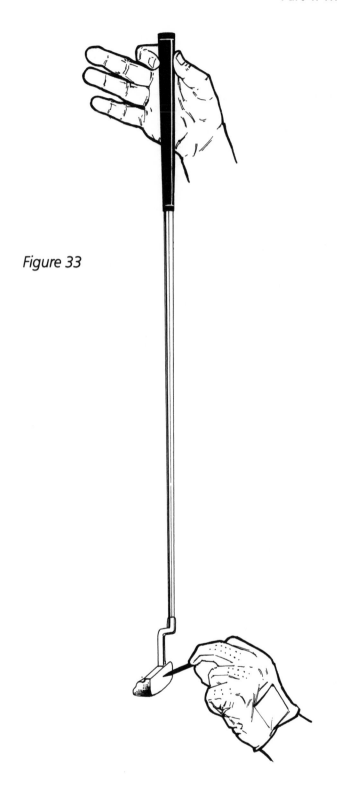

Figure 33

Remember, putting is the one place in golf where everyone can cut strokes. There is a lot of truth to the saying that you "drive for show and putt for dough." Start spending more of your practice time on your short game. Make the putting green your principle practice area. I promise you will see the results in lower scores.

Part 5
How To Prepare Yourself To Play Your Best

19 The Value of Proper Equipment

If they don't fit, don't use them

There is one area of the game that affects every shot that your play—your equipment. Before you step on the first tee, you need to make some very complex decisions about what type of clubs will suit you best. For example, you need to decide whether to use forged- or investment-cast irons. Should you use pro models or heel-and-toe weighted clubs? What mix of clubs should make up your set? What about shaft-flex and swingweight? The list of types of clubs and personal specifications goes on and on.

Another important decision you must make is what type of ball to use. Balata or surlyn? Three-piece or two-piece construction? What about dimple configuration? These equipment decisions can get very technical. You may say, "I'm not good enough to get this technical." Well, I am going to say bluntly and emphatically that whether you are a 30-handicapper or a scratch player, it cannot hurt to get some professional technical advice about what is best for you. Using properly fitted equipment and a ball with aerodynamic qualities that best fit your abilities and flight pattern can do nothing but help you. Every one of us can use all the help we can get. And if all these variables did not matter, club and ball manufacturers would not spend so much money on research and development in order to make so many different models of clubs and balls.

Properly fitted clubs will automatically help you because if a club is the right fit, it places your body in its optimum position for producing a balanced, controlled and powerful swing. The following analogies help prove the point. First, what good would it be to own a beautiful Rolls Royce or Mercedes if the seats were not adjustable or you could not reach the pedals or slide back for needed legroom? Second, what good is an immaculate five-hundred-dollar suit if the jacket is way too big, or the pants legs are too long or too short? Sure you would love to have a Rolls Royce and an expensive suit, but it would be neither practical nor functional if they did not fit.

Golf clubs are the same. Whether you pay a hundred or a thousand dollars for them, your golf clubs are only functional if they fit *you*. Unfortunately, many players, a percentage I fear is too big to venture even a guess, are playing with clubs that are not correct for them. They are playing at a big disadvantage. They are behind the eight ball, so to speak.

Once I have brought someone to this point the next statement I usually hear is, "Well, I'm average height so I guess I should use standard clubs," or "I'm tall so I need long clubs," or "I'm short so I should use short clubs." I usually respond to these statements, which may or may not be correct, by asking what "standard" actually means. The specifications for clubs that are considered "standard" are just a starting point that the companies use based on data that tell them what will come closest to fitting the greatest percentage of players. But we are all different, and we all need to be measured for that perfect fit. Three people can be of identical height, but if each has different length arms each will need different length clubs, different lies and maybe even different grip sizes.

You are probably now asking, "How can I get measured for the proper equipment?" The answer is simple: go see your PGA professional. Most professionals are relatively proficient at clubfitting, but as in any profession, there are some who are simply superior in this area of expertise. Ask around at courses in your area for recommendations and references, then go see the one who tops the list.

The club manufacturers themselves are another source of information. They provide questionnaires that ask you to list your most relevant body specifications—height, weight, distance from your fingertips to the ground, glove size and other points. They also ask you how far you hit the ball with various clubs and the flight pattern of your shots. Then they make recommendations on clubs based on the data you supply. The only problem with this procedure is that the manufacturer cannot see you set up to the ball. Although your "on paper" specifications may call for one club, you may actually need something slightly different. This is why I feel that the personal touch of an experienced professional checking you over is the best way to go. He can use his experience to measure you and, if need be, adjust the club specs a little to better fit you if, for whatever reason, what the charts recommend does not really look right for you.

I hope by now you are convinced that properly fitted clubs are a definite asset that will improve your game. Now let's list some of the most important variables of clubfitting that you should know about and check. They are shaft length, shaft-flex, the lie of the club and the grip size.

The shaft is the most important part of the club, so both its length and flex must be right. The length of the shaft is important because it can directly affect your posture at address and throughout your swing. Clubs that are too short for you (based on the distance from your fingertips to the ground while standing erect) will cause you to stoop and reach. Thus they invite poor balance during your swing. Clubs with shafts that are too long force you to choke up on the grip. You might stand too tall with your weight back on your heels causing stiffness. Again, poor balance will result.

The amount of flex in the shaft is very important because it is directly responsible for the flight pattern (draw, fade or straight) and the flight trajectory, meaning the takeoff pattern and height your shots attain. Shafts that are too stiff usually cause low shots that slide to the right and feel very "hard" at impact. Too weak or flexible a shaft causes pop-ups and directional problems. A player who tells me he feels he makes good swings but that the ball can curve in either direction is most likely using shafts that are too weak or too flexible.

The lie of the club can best be described as the way the club sits on the ground at address. The proper lie for any golfer is one in which the sole of the club lies flat on the ground when the player is holding it in his standard address position. When the toe of the club is in the air at address, the club is too upright for you. Likewise, if the heel is off the ground at address, the lie is too flat for you. In my experience, more golfers are playing with clubs that are too upright (toe off the ground at address) than with clubs that are too flat. Either way, your club professional can make the proper adjustments if he has a lie and loft machine, or he can have the adjustments done for you by an expert in club repair.

The lie is important because it affects the alignment of the clubface at impact. When a club is toed up, the heel hits the ground first at impact so that it is slowed up and the toe catches up and turns over, closing the face. The result is a hooked or pulled shot that usually flies low. If the club's heel is up at impact, the toe hits the ground first, causing the face to open and the ball to be sliced or blocked. A properly soled club strikes the ground evenly along the blade so that the club stays square through impact.

Grip size is an underrated but very important equipment factor. You cannot grip the club properly if you do not have the proper grip thickness to work with. Your grips are the right size if the tips of your middle, ring and little fingers on your left hand just brush up against the pad of your palm below the thumb. Your grips are too small if your fingers curl under the thumb pad. The latter causes your left hand to roll over to the right on the grip into a strong position. And as you know, a strong left hand causes both hands to become overactive in the impact zone, releasing too much so that the shot is hooked. Grips that are too thin can also lead to too much tension in your hands, arms and shoulders since you have to squeeze too hard to hold the club. Too much tension causes you to hold or stop the release, so that a slice or a blocked shot becomes likely.

One shot can go left, the next one right, all because your grips are too thin. "Army" golf, as I call this left-right action, is for the birds. If your fingernails curl under your thumb pad you need to get your grips built up. Your club pro or club repair specialist can assist you in determining just how much more size you need.

The other side of the coin is a grip that is too thick for your hands. This grip causes underactivity of the hands because your grip or hold on the club is inadequate. Shots tend to be sliced or blocked to the right. It is a problem easily remedied by installing thinner grips.

These four variables—shaft length, shaft-flex, lie and grip size—are the four most important physical specifications in club fitting. Correcting problems in any of these areas will significantly help your swing and add consistency to your game.

Now that I have discussed clubfitting, let's cover a few more points about golf equipment that are important for you to be aware of.

Many golfers are befuddled about the terms "forged" and "cast" irons. Forged irons are made of softer metals and are commonly referred to as "Tour model" clubs. These clubs usually have smaller heads, smaller sweet spots and a smaller margin for error on off-center hits. Thus, the classic forged designs are probably more suited to professionals and low-handicap amateurs.

Investment-cast irons are made of a much harder metal than forged irons, so their feel at impact is not quite as smooth. Cast irons are invariably weighted more at the heel and the toe than are forged clubs. The heel and toe weighting concept means that weight has been displaced (these clubs usually have some sort of cavity at the back), so that more weight is out at the toe, and the sweet spot, or most effective hitting area, is expanded. The weight is also set lower in the clubhead, which helps add height to your shots.

Investment-cast irons are also usually offset at the hosel or neck so that as you look down, the shaft is slightly ahead of the clubface. This difference gives the club an extra fraction of a second to square up and reduces any tendency to push or slice. The purpose of heel- and toe-weighted clubs is to provide all the technological advances of modern science to aid you, the golfer. If you do not already have a set you may want to test one. I am sure you will find that you will hit the ball straighter and, yes, longer too.

A relatively recent equipment question has arisen over the list of lightweight versus regular-weight clubs. The newest scientific advances have brought us the "ultralight" clubs, which have swingweights in the "B" range as opposed to the "D" swingweighted clubs used by most male golfers.

The lightweight clubs are great in the hands of the right player. The principle behind them is simply that they are very light and thus easier to swing while developing more clubhead speed. It is a wonderful innovation for players who are of lesser strength, have lost some flexibility or have any disabling condition. Seniors, ladies and still-developing juniors are players who should consider using these clubs.

A common complaint about lightweight clubs concerns their lack of "feel." Many physically strong players claim that the club is so light that they cannot feel the clubhead and know where it is throughout the swing. All things considered, however, the ultralight clubs definitely have merit. The best advice I can give is to hit some balls with them and see if they work for you. Perhaps you can take a set on a "test run" on the course. Again, see your pro and he will help you make all the right choices.

You hear a lot of talk about a golf club's swingweight, but what does this term mean? Swingweight is a system or method or code that was created for the purpose of identifying and matching all the clubs in a set to the same weight characteristic. Swingweight is defined as the weight of the head versus the rest of the club, that is , the shaft and grip. It is identified by a letter and a number—the farther into the alphabet and the higher the number, the heavier the swingweight. For example, a club swingweighted at C3 will feel heavier than a B4, but certainly lighter than a D2.

I believe that swingweight is really one of the least important variables in clubfitting. The reason I have mentioned it is because it is really about the only one most people know or at least have heard about. They may not understand it, but they know the term and unfortunately abuse it. After all, the difference between one swingweight point and the next is an amount equivalent to the weight of two dollar bills. Moving from a D1 to a D2 swingweight is of minimal importance, although if you were to move all the way into the ultralight or "B" swingweight range, the change would be really significant.

The following chart will help guide you with regard to the swingweight range you should be using:

Swingweight Range	Player
B2-C2 (ultralights)	Relatively weak players *and* those who like the feel of an extra-light club
C2-C6	Seniors, ladies, juniors
C7-DO (usually graphite or lightweight steel shafts)	Middle-handicap male players and stronger women
D2-D6 (usually dynamic shafts)	Professionals and lower-handicap men

What about the debate that is raging over metal versus wood? In recent years, metal "woods" have invaded the world or golf and have seriously threatened the sanctity of persimmon and laminated woods. Metal woods are made with the same design characteristics of the heel- and toe-weighted irons. They are definitely easier to hit both higher and straighter. They do not necessarily hit the ball farther. In fact, most professionals feel that the "wood" woods are longer.

Graphite-headed clubs make the same claim to being straighter, but they also claim added length. There may be something to it, but these clubs have not been on the market long enough for anyone to be sure. My recommendation is that you try all of them and see what works best for you.

As you probably know, you are allowed to carry a maximum of fourteen clubs in your set. But you have a wide variety of choices as to which fourteen provide the best combination for you. Within your own set, you may want to have some variations available so that you will be suited for any course you play or for varying weather conditions.

As a rule of thumb, junior golfers, seniors, ladies and higher handicap men should lean toward the lofted fairway and utility woods rather than the 2- and 3-irons. These golfers are not likely to generate enough clubhead speed to hit the long irons very well, so a more useful set for this group of golfers is 1-, 3-, 5-, 6- and 7-woods, and the 4-iron through the sand wedge. The putter is the fourteenth club.

Slightly stronger players may drop the 7-wood and carry the 3-iron instead. Then again, there are many strong-hitting amateurs who need carry only three woods, and who should include the 2- and 3-iron in their bags. Golfers in all categories might find a lofted third wedge beneficial at the expense of one of the long irons.

Again, talk with your pro. He knows your game. With input on your strengths and weaknesses, how you would like to fly the ball and the characteristics of your course, he can recommend the best combination for you.

There is a tremendous number of choices of golf balls available to the consumer today. The player's first choice must be the material used for the ball's cover: balata versus surlyn. Balata is a genuine rubber cover that has been used for decades. Balata-covered balls are also known as "three-piece" balls: they are made of a core surrounded by winding, the pressure of which determines the compression of the ball. The thin balata cover surrounds the winding. Balata offers more feel and spin, although it also has the undesirable characteristic of cutting when it is mishit. Good amateurs and professionals like balata balls because they feel better at impact and because the spin lets them maneuver or curve the ball at will. Because a balata ball spins better than a surlyn ball, it flies higher and lands softer with less roll. These are all performance qualities that a ball must have for a really good golfer to use it.

Surlyn, meanwhile, is a synthetic plastic cover that was invented to give a golf ball more durability. The majority of surlyn balls are two-piece balls; a hard one-piece center is underneath the cover. Usually, surlyn covers are much thicker than balata covers. Consequently, these balls spin less, fly a little lower and roll more. They also do not cut and scrape as readily as balata balls do. All of these are playing characteristics that the vast majority of amateur golfers need.

Some surlyn balls are also made with a three-piece construction. These are balls with the inside construction of balata balls, but which are covered with the harder surlyn. What you have here is a nice mixture of durability and feel. A large number of golfers like the durability of the two-piece ball but still want some of the feel and spin characteristics of a three-piece balata ball.

If you are confused about the right ball for you, the following chart will help guide you:

Cover material and construction	Type of golfer who will benefit
Balata (three-piece)	Professionals, low-handicap amateurs, long hitters
Surlyn (three-piece)	Middle-handicap males, low-handicap ladies, anyone who wants a combination of durability and performance
Surlyn (two-piece)	Ladies, juniors under 14, higher handicappers, anyone else who seeks durability and added roll on his or her shots

Have I left out something regarding equipment? I think so, because I have noticed that a high percentage of golfers play without wearing a glove on their left hand (for right-handed players). I recommend that every golfer wear a good leather glove. It will definitely make your hold on the club more secure, particularly in warmer weather when perspiration can become a real problem.

By now, you have learned a great deal about long and short game techniques, about strategy and about equipment. You are nearly ready to go out and play your best game of golf ever. But in the final chapter, I want to talk to you some more about what you will need to put it all together.

20 Constructing a Total Game

How to be a high quality practicer

We have all heard the expression, "Practice makes perfect." Now, everyone understands that they cannot attain perfection at the game of golf, because that would mean knocking the ball in the hole every time it was within reach. Even a golf-ball-hitting robot could not possibly do that. However, we can certainly become better and more consistent.

There is a golf professional I know who has a picture in his office that tells the story in a nutshell. It is a picture of a bucket of range balls with a club lying on top of it. The caption reads, "The Answer." Well, this is most of the story. But first you must have specific knowledge of what you want to accomplish in your practice sessions, whether it be improving a segment of your swing, developing a different flight pattern or reading your putts better. Then you must get down to the hard work required.

Every player needs to learn what amount and what kind of practice is best for him. On the range, you should always start with the short irons and work your way through the set up to the woods. This progression allows you to increase your flexibility slowly and to avoid muscle strains or pulls.

From the first swing you make on the practice tee, you should always be aiming at a target. After all, golf is a target-oriented sport. The object of the game is to hit the ball as close to the hole as possible, with the ultimate goal being to hit it in the hole. Yet few golfers take care about their alignment on every practice shot. Poor or careless alignment is an easy trap to fall into, more so on the practice range than anywhere else. The biggest abuse of this basic tenet occurs when golfers practice their wood shots. Most head for the range, pull out their driver and begin firing away. They neither take aim nor work up to a full driver swing. Remember, you will hit the woods better if you loosen up with the irons first.

Rule number one, then, is always to use a target. Rule number two is to hit a higher percentage of iron shots when you practice, particularly early in the session. It is important that your practice sessions be meaningful and productive.

You must work to hit every practice shot intelligently, taking your time, so that you do not simply become a "ball beater." Play games with yourself on the practice tee. Make believe you are playing in your club championship or the U.S. Open. Visualize a flagstick and the shot you need to hit, then do it. Work on your setup routine for each shot, because this is the place to get it grooved. Another useful practice aid is to keep changing your target. This way you do not get zeroed in on one area, and you must adjust your body and clubface alignment constantly. You want to groove your swing, but you also need the ability to adjust from shot to shot.

One point I should stress here is that all practice and no play makes Jack a poor player. Remember, you have to be able to take your swing from the range out onto the course. After all, you do not want to be the kind of player I call a "range jockey"—a player who looks good on the range but cannot produce a score. So play as much as possible, because the real test of your golf swing is the ability to make it work on the course. Play by yourself, and try different shots to see what works best for you.

Here is a practice aid I use when playing that really helps my game. I hit two balls from tee to cup and always play from the spot of my worst shot of the two. Believe me, it is a tough exercise! But it sure improves your ability to grind on every shot, because in this format, one great shot and one bad one does you no good. Naturally, it also helps you improve your short game as you scramble around the greens trying to get the ball up and down.

Another playing tip is to play with better players as much as you possibly can. Watch what they do, how they do it and how they handle themselves. Do not be afraid to ask them why they hit a certain shot and how they hit it. You will be surprised how many of them will graciously talk to you and help you. Remember that everyone has an ego and will take your request for information as a compliment.

But back to the tasks of the practice tee. One thing you must learn with certainty from your practice is the average distance you hit every club. Sure you do not hit it perfectly every time, and your distances vary. But every shot to a green has a yardage that must be covered to get there, and the only way you can hit a good shot onto the green is to make a good swing after selecting the correct club.

The best way to learn your distances is to hit thirty to forty balls with each club (you will probably need more than one session to do a really thorough job). Use good balls for this test. Throw out your longest and shortest hits. Then walk to the center of the bunch that makes up your "average" shots, carefully counting your step. Now you know your average length with that club. Remember that it is always best to measure your shots under normal wind and temperature conditions.

When you are out on the course, you will run into different conditions that you must "factor in" to select the right club. Let's say there's a breeze in your face. First figure out your yardage to the pin. Then decide if the wind will add one, two or even three clubs to the shot. Then you subtract that number from the club needed for the basic yardage you have to cover. If it is a two-club wind against you, what is normally a 6-iron shot becomes a 4-iron shot. Make the wind and add-on or a deduction from every club selection.

The majority of high handicappers are consistently short of the flag with their approach shots for two reasons. First, they work on the assumption that they will hit their "career" shot every time, instead of their average one as they should. Second, they usually think they hit the ball much farther than they actually do. They may *think* they can hit a 5-iron 170 yards, when in reality they are hard-pressed to hit it 150. It is no crime to hit a 5-iron 140 hards or 130 yards. You can still hit good golf shots and score well. But it is silly to tell yourself you can do something you cannot. Do not fall for this delusional kind of thinking. Be objective. Learn the average length you hit each club and pay close attention to your yardages when you are on the course.

When discussing ways to improve through practice, we should include some ideas about whether or not you should take lessons. Although I hope that this book will improve your game in all areas, I also believe that the best way to improve is to take lessons from your PGA professional. Golf is a science that requires ongoing study. Also, you cannot see yourself playing the game and falling into errors, so seeing a pro is the best approach toward improvement.

Choosing your professional instructor is important. Do not entrust your game to just anybody. Ask your friends for recommendations and comments and choose the pro who is most highly recommended. Once you select one, give him your best effort. Stick with him and give him a chance to explain full what he would like you to do and why. Many players, if they do not shoot a career round the next time out, simply run off to another pro. They do themselves much more harm than good because they confuse themselves.

Golf is a continuous learning experience, and improving can be a long, slow process. You must realize that learning to play golf well takes time—even years—and it is a learning process that never ends. So be fair to yourself and to your pro and give the learning process time, effort and patience.

The playing lesson is one of the most overlooked learning tools in golf, both by pros and by students. A playing lesson simply means that you play a 9- or 18-hole round with your pro, during which he advises you on all aspects of your play. You work with an expert on strategy, club and shot selection, course management and the mental side of the game. You do not work on the mechanics of your swing during a playing lesson. Save that for the practice tee. The point of a playing lesson is to ingrain all those intangibles that help you get the ball into the hole in the least possible number of strokes. Taking playing lessons is smart—it means you are getting in tune with thinking, "It's not how but how many"—the mark of a good golfer.

You should keep records and charts of your performance in all categories of the game. We have just talked about the need to practice and to make your practice worthwhile. Therefore, your best practice will be your practice on the areas you are *not* handling well. Keeping records and charts on your playing performance will tell you without a doubt where your strong and weak points lie. Sometimes a player simply does not realize that his wedge play is killing him. Or he may not know that the reason he hits so few greens in regulation is that he misses practically every fairway with the driver.

You can set up a chart to record whatever you want to know. Here is a sample chart:

Date	May 20	May 23	May 28
Location	Quail Creek	Stonington	Quail Creek
Score	88	93	86
Fairways hit	6	7	8
Fairways missed left	2	3	2
Fairways missed right	6	4	4
Greens in regulation	7	4	6
Penalty strokes	2	3	0
Up and down from fringe	1 of 5	0 of 4	2 of 4
Up and down from traps	1 of 3	0 of 2	0 of 1
Total putts	36	36	32
Putts missed left	8	6	6
Putts missed right	5	4	3
Putts missed short	5	8	5

Make your chart, fill it in after each round, and use it to plan your practice sessions. It is a good idea to color-code your chart with different color markers. Set up a rating, based on a realistic assessment of your game, of what is excellent, good, fair or poor performance for you in each category. For example, if hitting eleven greens in regulation is excellent for you, record that number in your "excellent" color. If you took thirty-seven putts and consider that poor (as you should), mark that number in your "poor" color. Pretty soon your patterns of strong and weak points will become obvious at a glance.

Keep records and use them to schedule your practice. Remember, work hardest on what needs improving, but do not neglect completely what is still good.

I think that about does it. If you have read this book carefully, you now have an understanding of the total picture of what golf is and how it should be played. You now need to set your own goals and decide your degree of dedication to improvement. Then commit yourself to the necessary course of action to achieve and maintain that standard. Be honest with yourself and set goals that are realistic, that are within the reach of your mental and physical abilities in a given time frame. When you reach these goals, you can set new ones that are a little higher. With all this in mind, and using a fundamental approach, look for your game to improve in terms of enjoyment, satisfaction and score.